Hedgehog

Animal
Series editor: Jonathan Burt

Already published

Albatross Graham Barwell · *Ant* Charlotte Sleigh · *Ape* John Sorenson · *Bear* Robert E. Bieder
Bee Claire Preston · *Camel* Robert Irwin · *Cat* Katharine M. Rogers · *Chicken* Annie Potts
Cockroach Marion Copeland · *Cow* Hannah Velten · *Crocodile* Dan Wylie · *Crow* Boria Sax
Deer John Fletcher · *Dog* Susan McHugh · *Dolphin* Alan Rauch · *Donkey* Jill Bough
Duck Victoria de Rijke · *Eel* Richard Schweid · *Elephant* Dan Wylie · *Falcon* Helen Macdonald
Fly Steven Connor · *Fox* Martin Wallen · *Frog* Charlotte Sleigh · *Giraffe* Edgar Williams
Gorilla Ted Gott and Kathryn Weir · *Hare* Simon Carnell · *Hedgehog* Hugh Warwick
Horse Elaine Walker · *Hyena* Mikita Brottman · *Kangaroo* John Simons · *Leech* Robert G. W. Kirk
and Neil Pemberton · *Leopard* Desmond Morris · *Lion* Deirdre Jackson · *Lobster* Richard J. King
Monkey Desmond Morris · *Moose* Kevin Jackson · *Mosquito* Richard Jones · *Octopus* Richard Schweid
Ostrich Edgar Williams · *Otter* Daniel Allen · *Owl* Desmond Morris · *Oyster* Rebecca Stott
Parrot Paul Carter · *Peacock* Christine E. Jackson · *Penguin* Stephen Martin · *Pig* Brett Mizelle
Pigeon Barbara Allen · *Rabbit* Victoria Dickenson · *Rat* Jonathan Burt · *Rhinoceros* Kelly Enright
Salmon Peter Coates · *Shark* Dean Crawford · *Snail* Peter Williams · *Snake* Drake Stutesman
Sparrow Kim Todd · *Spider* Katja and Sergiusz Michalski · *Swan* Peter Young · *Tiger* Susie Green
Tortoise Peter Young · *Trout* James Owen · *Vulture* Thom van Dooren · *Whale* Joe Roman
Wolf Garry Marvin

Hedgehog

Hugh Warwick

REAKTION BOOKS

To Zoe, Mati and Pip – and all the hedgehogs
who have made this work possible.

Published by
REAKTION BOOKS LTD
33 Great Sutton Street
London EC1V 0DX, UK
www.reaktionbooks.co.uk

First published 2014
Copyright © Hugh Warwick 2014

Printed and bound in China by Toppan Printing Co., Ltd

A catalogue record for this book is available from the British Library

ISBN 978 1 78023 275 1

Contents

1 What is a Hedgehog?

Few mammals are as immediately identifiable as the hedgehog. The defensive coat of spines certainly makes the job of identification simpler but it is not unique. In fact, there are many animals which protect themselves with similar prickly defences.

The most frequent error people make is to assume that a relationship exists between the porcupine and the hedgehog. The porcupine is a rodent, from the mammalian order Rodentia, which contains, for example, rats, mice, squirrels and beavers. In contrast, the hedgehog is of the order Eulipotyphla, recently placed there after the order Insectivora, under which it had previously been classified, was abandoned (Insectivora had, for generations, been used as a taxonomic dumping ground for many small, relatively unspecialized, primitive-looking insectivorous mammals that did not seem to fit anywhere else.) Porcupines are also much bigger than hedgehogs and, to be honest, look nothing like them.

Other spiny mammals exist too: mice and rats. The mice, of the genus *Acomys*, are not as well protected as the hedgehog; they have rather robust guard hairs rather than a coat of prickles. But this gives an indication of the origin of spines – they are simply modified hairs.

Far more hedgehog-like than rats, mice and porcupines are the tenrecs. Confined to Madagascar and the Comoro Islands,

Hystrix Dorn schwein stachel schwein

Herinaceus Igel Sewin Igel

Hedgehogs and porcupines are very different creatures, and even when the illustrations look nothing like what they are supposed to, the differences are clear. It is possible that Joannes Jonstonus, who put together the *Historiae naturalis libri* in 1657, had never set eyes on either beast.

the two species have names that suggest similarity: the lesser hedgehog tenrec, *Echinops telfairi*, and the greater hedgehog tenrec, *Setifer setosus*. These do indeed look more hedgehog-like, at first glance anyway, although on closer inspection they are very different: the tenrec's spines extend to cover its broad tail, unlike the hedgehog whose tail is short, slightly hairy and spine-free.

The tenrecs are also more arboreal than the hedgehog, spending time in trees as well as on the ground. And while they have some capacity to defend themselves in the typical hedgehog manner by rolling into a ball, they do not have the same specialized musculature that enables the hedgehog to maintain such an effective defensive posture. Additionally, tenrecs are cloacal: the anus and the urogenital tracts share a single opening, a feature more commonly found in birds, reptiles and amphibians.

Finally there are the echidnas, also known as spiny anteaters. These are a class apart, being monotremes – egg-laying mammals – from Australasia. Along with the duck-billed platypus, they are the only mammals to lay eggs. They look rather different to hedgehogs; they are stocky, strong-limbed and have distinctive snouts. The short-beaked echidna, for example, is much larger than the hedgehog at up to 45 cm long and weighs up to 5 kg. They are also thought to be the hosts of the world's largest flea – *Bradiopsylla echidnae* – which is 4 mm long.

Hedgehog spines, like the spines that cover all the animals mentioned above, are modified hairs. In the hedgehog they look like magnified hairs, with a bulb embedded into the skin, and a thin section – starting as the spine emerges from the skin – that is slightly angled and then broadens out before tapering to a sharp point at the tip. Among the spines across the back of the hedgehogs, there are no ordinary hairs, and the spines do not extend

A lesser hedgehog tenrec (*Echinops telfairi*), endemic to Madagascar, displays many hedgehog-like characteristics, while being a very different sort of mammal.

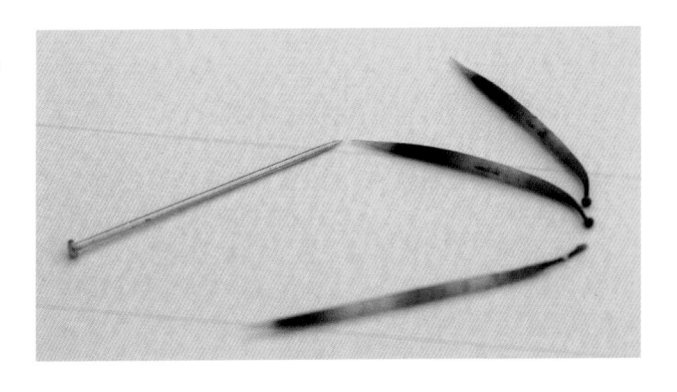

beyond the crown of the head and the base of the tail. On the flanks the spines seem to reach the ground when the animal is still but it becomes clear that there is a 'skirt' of spines that is lifted, revealing surprisingly long legs, when quicker locomotion is required; in fact, the hedgehog can reach speeds of up to 9 km an hour, the equivalent of a brisk human walk.

That 'skirt' of spines is necessary to provide the extra coverage of defensive skin when the hedgehog retreats into its characteristic ball. The ball-rolling is achieved at first with a frown. A muscle similar to the one humans use to frown extends on hedgehogs from the forehead to the tail. That muscle can pull the spines on the forehead forward, defending the face, and cause the spines along the back to bristle.

If a threat is perceived to remain, the job of rolling up begins. While other animals can and do roll themselves up, none manage it with the brilliance of the hedgehog.[1] One pair of muscles pulls the skin down over the head, another pair does the same with the bottom, and then a muscle named the *orbicularis* tightens, sealing the hedgehog within its spines (the *orbicularis* is a thickened circular ridge of muscle that runs around the body and when contracted acts rather like a drawstring). This position can

When a hedgehog needs to walk with any speed, it will hitch up a 'skirt' of muscle and reveal legs longer than one might expect.

An African hedgehog feeling cautious; its spines are pulled a little forward over the head.

An African hedgehog feeling more threatened, pulling its spines right over the face, the final step before forming a protective ball.

be maintained for hours; the animal is relaxed apart from the tension in the *orbicularis*.

The spines have an obvious role in defence, but are also valuable as shock absorbers. The slender angled section allows the spine to flex, preventing it from being driven back into the body of the animal should it fall. But it is their defensive role that makes hedgehogs so unmistakable and so iconic.

The modern hedgehog has evolved from the earliest shrew-like mammals that first emerged while the dinosaurs still held sway. The fossil record for Eulipotyphla extends back to the end of the Cretaceous period (145–66 million years ago, MYA). This would suggest that there were hedgehog-like animals scurrying around the planet while dinosaurs still held sway. Fossils we can link directly to our modern-day hedgehogs have emerged from Asia and date back to the Eocene period (56–33.9 MYA). It is thought that hedgehogs spread through Africa, Europe and North America during the Miocene (23–5.3 MYA).[2]

One of these Miocene hedgehogs is *Deinogalerix*, an extinct hedgehog that roamed what is now southern Italy some 24 million years ago. The Natural History Museum in London has produced an artist's impression of this early hedgehog, which weighed 9 kg – as large as a Cocker spaniel. Its name means 'terrible shrew'; the root, *deino*, meaning terrible, as it does in

Albino hedgehog.

'dinosaur', 'terrible lizard'. But even before this monstrous animal was abroad, hedgehogs had undergone a split that remains to this day: the subfamily that *Deinogalerix* belonged to, the Galericinae or 'hairy hedgehogs', had emerged.

Our definition of hedgehogs as spiny animals, as opposed to hairy ones, is of our own making; evolution is not as bothered by appearance. Six species of hairy hedgehogs, including gymnures and moonrats, live in the moist jungles of Southeast Asia. They look superficially like rats, with the largest, the greater moonrat, weighing up to 1.4 kg. But they are nonetheless eulipotyphlans, like hedgehogs, shrews, desmans and moles. The gymnures and moonrats lack spines but are equipped with an alternative defensive strategy: malodorous anal glands that make the animal smell of garlic, sweat and rotten onions.

Deinogalerix koenigswaldi was a giant hairy hedgehog. This fossil (from South Gargano, Italy, 25–2.5 million years old) is on display in the National Museum of Natural History in Leiden, The Netherlands.

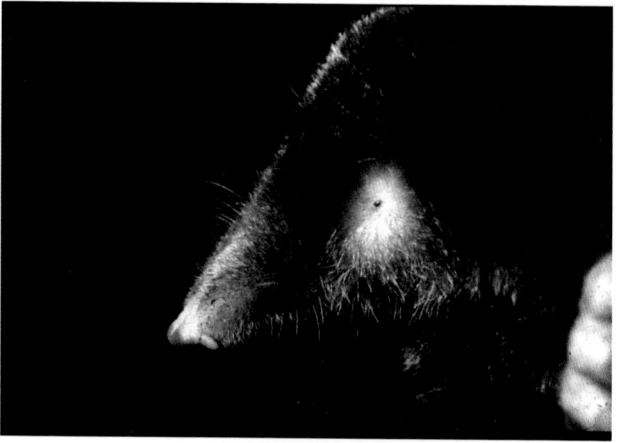

Moles (*Talpa europaea*) are closely related to hedgehogs.

Erinaceus europaeus. Common Hedgehog.

Talpa europæa. Common Mole.

Both hedgehogs and moles were part of the Insectivora – until taxonomists shifted them into the Eulipotyphlans. Engraving from 1890.

Very little is known about the Galericinae, and that is all the attention they will receive in this book. Instead, we will be concentrating solely on the species of spiny hedgehog native to Africa and Eurasia. There is some debate over the exact number of different species of spiny hedgehog around the world, but the best review concludes that there are fourteen.[3] These are split between four genera, based on both phenotypes (how they look) and karyotypes (their genetic make-up).

Gymnures, tenrecs and hedgehogs have long been associated with each other. These engravings from 1854 lump them together, despite tenrecs being from a different taxonomic order.

HEDGEHOGS AROUND THE WORLD

First, *Erinaceus*. The bulk of this book is going to be concerned with the species about which most is known, the Western European hedgehog or common hedgehog, *Erinaceus europaeus*. This species ranges from Ireland in the west to southern Scandinavia in the north and the Czech Republic in the east, where another species starts to be seen, *E. concolor*, the white-breasted or Eastern European hedgehog. *E. concolor* reaches Israel in the south, north of the Caspian and east to Novosibirsk, Russia. There is one other species in the genus: *E. amurensis*, the Amur hedgehog, native to China and Korea.

The potential for breeding between the two European species has been proven in captivity,[4] but with limited success, and it is not known to what extent it happens in the wild. The main difference between them is in the colour of the chest fur – paler in the eastern species – and in the mask, which is more distinctive in the western. There is also a slight difference in the length of the snout: that of the eastern species is longer. This led to farmers and gypsies thinking that they were able to distinguish between them, referring to the western, blunt-snouted 'dog' hedgehog and the longer, more pointed snout of the 'pig' hedgehog in the east. However, it seems likely that this distinction is little more than folklore, made as it is in areas where there is only one species present.[5]

The southern extent of the Western European hedgehog was rather extended in 1870 when the Acclimatisation Society of the recently colonized New Zealand sent a message back to England asking for help in making the country feel more like home. This was in part to meet desires for sport and for food, with rabbits and deer among the ecologically disastrous imports. But the Society also specifically requested hedgehogs, and so a pair was placed on the ship *Hydaspes* for the lengthy journey. More batches were sent, initially to comfort the colonists but later to work as pest control agents, feeding on slugs and snails in the new gardens of New Zealand.[6] The hedgehogs made themselves very much at home and were considered to be the most benign of introductions until their impact on native birds, insects and reptiles was noted. Now they are subject to control, including hedgehog-specific lethal traps.

The *Paraechinus* are desert hedgehogs that range from Morocco to India. They tend to have a conspicuous parting of spines on their head and also large ears that protrude from the surrounding spines. The spines themselves are of a different texture to European ones, being rough and grooved. Like the *Erinaceus*, there are three species of *Paraechinus* recognized: *P. aethiopicus* is the Ethiopian hedgehog, found from Morocco to the Arabian peninsula; *P. hypomelas*, or Brandt's hedgehog, ranges from Iran and Afghanistan to Pakistan; and the pale or Indian hedgehog, *P. micropus*, is found in southern Pakistan and India. These species are poorly known and little researched. They are smaller, at around half the weight of a European hedgehog.

The four species of *Atelerix* hedgehog are, barring a few exceptions on islands and the Mediterranean coast of France and Spain, African. *A. albiventris* is a white-bellied hedgehog, as the name suggests, and comes from a belt across central Africa from Ethiopia

Indian hedgehog.

and Tanzania to Nigeria. Smaller than the European species, samples from the wild all weighed less than 500 g, whereas it is not uncommon for *E. europaeus* to be double that. They also lack a fifth toe, the vestigial hallux, which gives them their common name: the 'four-toed hedgehog'.

Atelerix algirus, the North African or Algerian hedgehog, has spread, probably deliberately introduced from Algeria and Morocco to coastal Europe and islands such as the Canaries. *A. frontalis* is the Southern African hedgehog and ranges up as far as Zimbabwe and down through South Africa. There is still some debate over whether *A. sclateri*, found only in northern Somalia, is actually distinguishable from *A. albiventris*, as intermediate forms have been identified.

Finally, the *Hemiechinus*, which like *Paraechinus* are long-eared and range from the Middle East and northern Africa to China. They have no central parting of spines on their crown and, unlike *Atelerix* and *Paraechinus* hedgehogs, there is no facial mask. *H. auritus* is known as the long-eared hedgehog. It is wide-ranging, preferring dry scrub, and is found from northern African to Mongolia. *H. collaris*, also known as Hardwicke's hedgehog, the Indian long-eared or the collared hedgehog, ranges from eastern Pakistan to northwestern India. Further east, the two remaining species are found, but remain very poorly studied: *H. dauricus*, the Daurian hedgehog, and *H. hughi*, or Hugh's hedgehog, both of which range across central China.

Unlike its lesser-studied siblings, there is a little known about the identification of Hugh's hedgehog, thanks to correspondence kept at London's Natural History Museum. In 1908 a paper was presented by Michael Oldfield Thomas, a prodigious collector who named over 2,000 animal species that were new to science. He described a hedgehog quite unlike any other that appeared to be very dark, with spines that were black at the tip. Oldfield

The long-eared hedgehog now known as *Hemiechinus auritus*, from Central Asia and the Middle East.

Der langöhrige Igel. (Erinaceus auritus. Lin.)

Thomas chose the name after the Franciscan missionary who had sent him the specimen, a Father Hugh from Hankow, China. The original skin, sent by Father Hugh to Oldfield Thomas, can still be found in the archive of the museum.

The distribution of all fourteen species clearly marks the hedgehog as an Old World creature. But they have not always been so restricted and did once roam the New World as well. For example, fossils of the extinct hedgehog genus *Brachyerix*, which lived during the Miocene between 5 and 20 million years ago, have been found in the Americas.[7]

The evolution of new species has been quite recent for some of the hedgehogs. Genetic scientists have been able to chart the way ice age events have contributed to our European species. As the ice fronts moved southwards across Europe, so fauna and flora were

Hedgehogs at a vineyard, Persia.

restricted into three main areas, the Iberian Peninsula, Italy and the Balkans. As the ice retreated, so hedgehogs were able to recolonize the continent, but did so as different species, *E. europaeus* and *E. concolor*.[8] So the cold climate contributed to the evolution of different species. It also allowed the hedgehog to develop a brilliant solution to the problems faced by all animals when the weather turns inclement.

HIBERNATION

The widespread presence of mammals with spiny defences raises the question of why this is not a feature shared across more mammals. The answer is that the spiny pelage requires a compromise. Defence against the attentions of a fox means the high-tog insulation of a fur coat is sacrificed. So while, for instance, a rabbit will be able to survive the chill of winter, and in fact can start breeding in the darkness of this season, the hedgehog is forced to adopt another strategy: hibernation.

Hedgehogs are not alone in shutting down during the winter; bats and dormice are the other British mammals that share the capacity. Hibernation is far more than a long and deep sleep. The need is to conserve energy. Being what is colloquially known as 'warm-blooded', that is, endothermic, hedgehogs need to generate their own internal heat through the metabolism of food. The hedgehog, unlike the rabbit, has a diet made up of food that vanishes as the temperature drops so, given the poor insulation provided by the spines, it needs to conserve energy. And this it does admirably.

Hibernation has long been a subject of fascination for scientists; initially they were just concerned with finding out how it worked, but more recently there has been research to see if there are any lessons to be learned that could be applied to human medicine. For example, the European Space Agency has been looking at the possibility of inducing hibernation in their astronauts to enable them to survive the lengthy journeys that interplanetary travel would require.[9]

Most of what is known about hedgehog hibernation comes from studies of the Western European hedgehog. As the hedgehog enters hibernation its body temperature drops from around 35°C to 10°C or lower, depending on the surroundings. The hedgehog continues to use a little energy to keep its body above freezing point, as freezing would be fatal. Because its metabolism is so slowed, and less oxygen is required to power the operation, there is a reduced need to breathe. Breathing can even halt for over an hour with no ill effects. And the heart rate – in the active animal up to 280 beats per minute; in a sleeping individual, about 150 – tumbles during hibernation to around five beats per minute. The hedgehog manages to survive on as little as 2 per cent of its usual energy requirements while in hibernation.

This is not a foolproof plan, however. Hedgehogs in hibernation are obviously vulnerable to predation and sudden changes in the environment around them, such as flooding or fires. Additionally, while the energy requirements are massively reduced, energy is still needed and stored energy will be consumed. Energy is stored in the form of fat, which the hedgehog needs to lay down in advance of the winter. This fat comes in two forms: the bulk of it is white fat, which provides the ticking-over fuel, while about 2 per cent of the body weight is made up of brown fat that serves as a sort of starter motor, helping to revive the hedgehog when hibernation is at its end.

Hedgehogs rarely spend the entire winter in deep hibernation, though they are quite capable of doing so. The triggers for entering and leaving hibernation are varied and not fully understood. Some are obvious, such as temperature. It is possible to keep a hedgehog out of hibernation by providing it with adequate food and maintaining the ambient temperature at around 17°C. And on North Island, New Zealand, the imported hedgehogs rarely hibernate at all.

This also reveals that hibernation is not a prerequisite for a healthy hedgehog. It is not like sleep. The amount of time spent in hibernation varies according to the environment. So at the north of its range, in Scandinavia, the Western European hedgehog will hibernate for around 200 days from October to April. In Britain it will often shave a month or more off those dates.

Interestingly, hibernation is not symmetrical across the sexes. Males enter hibernation earlier; they have not faced the same rigours of reproduction, having no involvement with the process following mating, so they have more time to feed themselves up to a suitable weight. The males are also the first to emerge from hibernation, with the purpose of preparing themselves for the courtship. These differences can be observed by anyone paying very close attention to the proportions of male and female hedgehogs found dead on the roads at the beginning and end of the active cycle.

During hibernation about 25 per cent of a hedgehog's body weight, in the form of fat, is consumed to keep it alive. This means that there is a minimum weight at which a hedgehog can enter hibernation and survive. And this observation has led to a great cottage industry of hedgehog rehabilitation as people take in underweight hedgehogs that would inevitably die during hibernation due to low fat reserves, and feed them up so they are fit for release in the spring.

The defence against the cold is not simply down to marvellous physiological adaptations. The nest-building skills of the hedgehog are frequently overlooked. Nest construction requires a supportive structure under which a hedgehog can collect vegetation, such as leaves and grass. The animal then rotates its body, combing the vegetation into layers of insulation. Studies have revealed that the constructions, known as hibernacula, can have great insulating qualities. Pat Morris, the world's leading hedgehog expert, found that a good nest can maintain an internal temperature of 1–5°C while the external temperature ranged from −8 to +10°C. This constant temperature range is crucial for surviving hibernation: protection from the cold is obviously important, but it is equally important that hedgehogs are not woken too often by warm spells. This is because they only have a finite amount of fuel to use as a starter motor, and too many arousals could use it all up before spring has truly sprung.[10] When there is a need to be aroused the hedgehog's store of brown fat is depleted, and when it is gone a hibernating hedgehog is simply waiting to die.

And so a good hibernaculum is the basis of a good hibernation. However, it is not the only type of hedgehog nest; there are also regular day nests which vary in construction from little more than a few leaves covering a resting hedgehog in woodland, to well-made and strong nests almost as detailed as a hibernaculum. Breeding nests have to be larger, to accommodate a litter of up to six offspring that will reach a weight of over 200 g each after six weeks, when it is time to strike out on their own.

These are just the most common kinds of nest. While hedgehogs are woodland-edge specialists, they can be found in many different habitats and will make use of what they can find. So, for example, they may well use rabbit holes where these abound. Similarly, desert hedgehogs of the *Hemiechinus* and *Paraechinus* genera will use existing vegetation and available holes and will also make their own burrows in soft soil. But in all cases, the hibernacula are clearly the most robust of the nests a hedgehog will use to provide protection for extended periods of time and while the hedgehog is, to a certain extent, insensate.

Interestingly, hibernation, from the Latin *hibernare* ('to winter') has a contrasting condition, aestivation (*aestivare*, 'to spend the summer'). Aestivation occurs in some species of hedgehog that live in hot and dry climates, and for very similar reasons to hibernation: seasonal fluctuation in the availability of food. In extremely hot and dry conditions the macro-invertebrate prey will secrete itself out of reach; so, to avoid starvation, hedgehogs reduce their need to consume food. Unfortunately very little is known about aestivation as it is not well studied.

The arousal of the hedgehog from hibernation has to coincide with the availability of hedgehog food. Across the range of species, diet is consistent in terms of the niche that the hedgehog is filling. Their diet tends to be macro-invertebrates though they can and do take a range of other prey. So while beetles, worms and caterpillars form the bulk of the stomach contents of a European hedgehog, they will also eat birds' eggs (which causes some not inconsiderable controversy), slugs (famously) and small mammals.

They will also sometimes attempt to tackle food that you wouldn't expect them to pursue. For example, a commotion was once heard coming from the small hen house of an Essex farm. On investigation the trouble was found to have been caused by a hedgehog that had managed to get hold of the foot of a chicken through the slats and was pulling with all its might. This hedgehog became one of the few to experience the sensation of flight as it was thrown by the farm owner into the neighbouring woodland.[11]

Indeed, hedgehog behaviour can often attract attention. Because so much of their lives take place out of our gaze, when they start to do something unexpected, people take note. For example, there is the strange business of self-anointing. Often, but not always, stimulated by a strong flavour or scent, a hedgehog will suddenly start to produce an excess of saliva which is worked into a froth with a smacking of lips and then spread far onto its back via its tongue and a good deal of quite remarkable contortion. But why? The suggestion was made by Pat Morris that self-anointing is stimulated by the chewing of the skin of a toad, which it can be. Perhaps, then, spreading saliva containing toad poison on to its spines would be the reason? But this theory is discounted, not least because of the wide range of innocuous

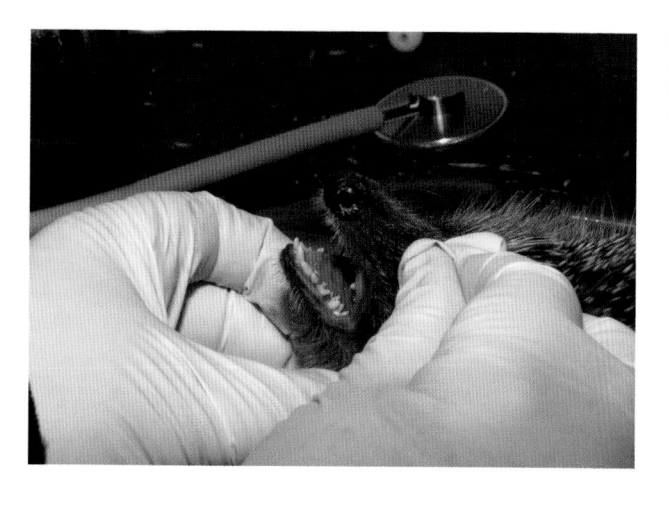

Hedgehog teeth are designed for catching small and often slippery prey.

substances that will generate such a response, ranging from soap to dog faeces, lavender bushes and distilled water. The most likely idea is to do with scent: perhaps there is a pheromone contained within the saliva, and the spreading of the saliva across the increased surface area of the spines helps it dissipate. But we still don't really know.[12]

The most regular upset caused by hedgehogs is down to sex, or at least courtship, even if the act is sometimes mistaken for something else, as reported in a letter to the British *Times* newspaper in 1933.[13] Having rescued a hedgehog from the churchyard, the correspondent 'brought him home and into the house, but vagrancy had unfitted him for ordinary society, so he ran out and into the garden'.

One evening, having gone to bed, we were disturbed to hear near us a noise as of an engine getting up steam. With a dog and a lantern we searched in the garden and found two hedgehogs fighting and using the most shocking

language. Horrified, we left them to find their own solution to what seemed such a very personal quarrel. They did. But, alas! next day one of them was dead – and the murderer made good his escape.

It is as likely that this quarrel was courtship. The comparison to an engine getting up to steam is a very clear description of the noise a female hedgehog makes to rebuff the advances of an amorous male. The process of courtship can be lengthy, with the male circling a fertile female, trying to get behind her, while she turns to face the potential intruder and occasionally forces him back with a plosive sneeze. This 'dance' is known as the 'Hedgehog Carousel'. Hours of noisy circling can bring plenty of attention, and also flatten vegetation in the area, which once led to the *Guardian* headline 'Hedgehogs Cleared of Corn Circle Dementia'.

The courtship of the hedgehog is frequently mistaken for violence, and this is probably why it has not been given vast amounts of attention, at least not in literature. But when it comes to the media, where members of the public are able to air their thoughts, the process of procreation becomes a far more celebrated event. It is likely that there has not been a year gone by without an article or letter appearing in a newspaper somewhere that goes like this:

> Two hedgehogs triggered a nocturnal police operation in Germany this week after the spiky little mammals awoke neighbours with their loud, shameless mating. They went on fornicating even as a crowd gathered to watch them. In fact the attention made them even more vigorous.
>
> Police called to investigate a disturbing noise in the garden of a house in Bremen, in northern Germany, were surprised to find it coming from two hedgehogs mating vigorously by a pond.[14]

Archibald Thorburn's print of two hedgehogs is far more realistic than many earlier images, though the mask on the one about to eat a beetle is a little darker than usual; 1912.

This particular story went international and was reported in the *China Daily* with the wonderful statement, '"The pair were loudly engaged in ensuring the continuity of their species", said Bremen police spokesman Ronald Walther.'

Mother and new-born hedgehogs.

The result of all this activity is, obviously, baby hedgehogs. In the UK most young hedgehogs are born in June and July, with a tendency for those in the north of the country to arrive a little later. Second litters are probably the result of the early loss of a first litter and, depending on when they arrive, can be at quite a disadvantage; the later in the year they are born, the less time there is for them to put on enough weight to survive hibernation.

Quite some care has to be taken with the process of birth because hedgehogs are born with spines. Fortunately for the females, the skin of the newborn is oedemic, that is, their spines are kept hidden by fluid that raises the skin enough to prevent injury. And this means that the newborn hedgehogs do not need to wait for spines to grow; to become protected they just need to wait for the fluid to be reabsorbed – a much quicker process.

These new spines are not as effective as an adult's, however; they are sparser, growing in two distinct patches, with a parting down the animal's backbone. White in colour, they are also much softer than their parents' spines. But they are a start. And they do not turn brown, as some observers have suggested. Brown spines grow through the white ones, which gradually fall out, as all spines do. The hedgehog does not moult as such – that could leave it vulnerable – but, as with human hair, there is a gradual turnover.

On average there are four or five young who stay with the mother for up to six weeks, feeding on milk for the first four from their mother's five pairs of nipples. They start to lose their milk teeth at this time and also begin to perform one of the cutest hedgehog events; just occasionally you might glimpse a convoy of mother hedgehog followed diligently by her young making their way across your garden.

Life is tough for the newborn hedgehog and one in five young do not make it out of the nest. Raising young is also a terrible strain on the mother, who will have fed the youngsters enough milk to raise their body weight to 250 g, ten times their birth weight.[15] And that is it for the family; once they leave the nest, hedgehogs are solitary animals and there is no evidence that

At five days old the white spines that emerge straight after birth are beginning to be overshadowed by the more mature, darker spines.

Hedgehog seen in profile; brush drawing in grey wash by Joseph Crawhall (1860–1913).

they relate differently to close blood relatives than to strangers later in life.

Most of what is known about the other species of hedgehog has been extrapolated from the studies of the Western European hedgehog. The lack of original research is at odds with the occurrence of scientific papers that appear when the search term 'hedgehog' is used. The reason? Hedgehog genes. Now it is hardly a shock that within a hedgehog there are hedgehog genes, but these are rather particular genes that we humans have within our own bodies. In fact there are 'hedgehog genes' in animals as diverse as fruit flies and chimpanzees. 'Hedgehog' is the name given to genes that mediate what is known as the 'hedgehog signalling pathway'. This pathway gives instructions to cells, enabling them to develop properly.

This gene was first identified in *Drosophila* – fruit flies – as crucial in the development of key differences, such as which cells become cells for the front and which for the back. All cells start from the same place: they grow from the union of sperm and egg. So there must be instructions to tell which cells to become what, and this is the great significance of the discovery. The name 'hedgehog' came from an experiment that created a mutant fruit fly with the gene switched off and resulted in embryos covered in small, tooth-like projections, resembling hedgehogs. And while the initial interest surrounded how the growing embryo actually manages to develop different components – head and tail, left and right – it was the pathway's connection with cancer that caused a great flurry of interest: malfunction of this genetic pathway has been linked with basal-cell carcinoma, among others.

For most people, however, their connection with the hedgehog is likely to be far more mundane. It is an animal that we encounter early on in our lives, either in the flesh or through the multitude of appearances in stories. And it is one, by dint of its appearance, that leaves a lasting impression.

2 Hedgehog Names and Folklore

It might be thought that the English name 'hedgehog' comes from the straightforward marrying of the observation of the animal's favourite habitat and its snuffling, hog-like manner. But there is another layer to the name, as 'hedge' itself is derived in part from the Middle High German *hagen*, which means thorn. The 'hog' component has also been attributed to the fact that the flesh tastes like pork, or that if you were to remove all the spines from a hedgehog, the bald animal looks remarkably like a baby wild boar.

The *Oxford English Dictionary* records the word *heyghoge* as first being used around 1450. The 1535 Coverdale Bible references the *hedghogge*, and this remained the accepted spelling until the nineteenth century when the modern word became the standard.

An earlier name for the hedgehog that is still in occasional use is 'urchin' (the sea urchin being an easily understood extension of that name). It seems likely that 'urchin' has its etymology in the Old Northern French word for hedgehog, *herichon*, which the *OED* finds evidence for in the twelfth century. And this word is clearly related to the modern-day French for the animal: *hérrison*. It is also possible that the old Romani name, *hotchi-witchi*, is at least in part derived from the same root.

Another old name for the animal is *il*, dating back to at least the ninth century. This can be linked to the current German,

Finding a hedgehog with alopecia is a rare event, for obvious reasons.

This Old Babylonian (20–16th century BC) hematite cylinder seal in the British Museum features a small hedgehog above the recumbent cow.

Why hedgehogs featured in burials of the Middle Kingdom remains far from certain. This green-glazed hedgehog from 1900–1800 BC has been carefully modelled.

Egyptian green-glazed cosmetic vessel in the form of a hedgehog, adorned with a human head (664–332 BC).

Dutch and Swedish words for hedgehog: *igel*, *egel* and *igelkott* respectively. The *kott* of the Swedish name refers to a pine cone. Denmark and Norway have similar names, *pindsvin* and *piggsvin*, where the prefixes *pind-* and *pigg-* translate as 'prickle', while the *svin* translates as 'pig' or 'hog'. Strangely, for such a charismatic beast, there are a series of Celtic names that refer to it as the 'horrible one' – *grainneog* (Irish), *crainneag* (Scottish Gaelic) and *draenog* (Welsh).

ANCIENT EGYPTIAN HEDGEHOGS

Whether noted for being horrible or prickly, the hedgehog has been recorded since the very earliest civilizations. And while it was never an animal to achieve royal status, it has been present since the Sumerians and the ancient Egyptians. So what is it culturally about the hedgehog that caused Egyptians during the Old Kingdom, between around 2649 and 2150 BC, to carve hedgehogs as figureheads on the prows of ships, facing back into the ship?[1] The reason for this remains a mystery.

Similarly difficult to explain is the appearance of hedgehogs in paintings of hunting scenes. The amateur Egyptologist André Dollinger put it rather well:

> Hunting was not without its risks. Wild bulls, elephants, crocodiles, hippos and lions were probably more dangerous than hedgehogs and partridges, but even hunting small prey was fraught with unforeseen dangers.

Still, it is hard to imagine many incidents of danger involving a hedgehog.

There is, however, some explanation for the popularity in ancient Egypt of amulets in the shape of hedgehogs. Cultures deeply wedded to the idea of reincarnation must have been fascinated by an animal that is seemingly able to die and be reborn: what other way would one describe the behaviour of a hibernating, or aestivating, hedgehog?[2]

Another of the hedgehog characteristics was also taken up as an indication that there might be some sympathetic benefit to be gained from representations of it; that is, its near-immunity to snake attack. There is a hedgehog-rattle, ceramic, hollow, blue and containing pellets, from the Middle Kingdom (c. 2000–1700 BC), that when shaken was used to ward off snakes, scorpions and malevolent spirits. In many snakes, the teeth are shorter than the spines of a hedgehog, so if a hedgehog is able to erect its prickles before the snake strikes, the

snake will simply injure itself, often repeatedly, until such time as it gives up and takes flight or is subdued enough to be eaten by the hedgehog. The impression is given of the hedgehog having immunity to the venom of the snake, and as such it can be accorded qualities that may be transferable on to people through sympathetic magic.

A woodcut of a viper and a hedgehog, 1490.

MEDICINAL HEDGEHOGS

The medicinal qualities of the hedgehog were also recognized by the ancient Egyptians. In the Ebers Papyrus from around 1550 BC it is argued that an amulet in the shape of one would confer protection against baldness. There is also reference in that document to the use of the spines, ground up and mixed with oil or fat, as a cure for the same condition.

Ceramic hedgehogs were not just used as rattles but also as oil containers; the hedgehog oil contained within them was reputed to have curative properties. The example in the Ashmolean Museum in Oxford shows a very round hedgehog with the spout just above the face of the stout animal. It was found in Abydos and dates to the Eighteenth Dynasty of the New Kingdom, which lasted from around 1550 BC to around 1295 BC. Hedgehog-shape oil jars were also used by the Greeks, and examples have been found in Corinth, Rhodes and Naukratis dating from the seventh century BC.

The use of hedgehog oil as a curative did not die with the ancients. The *Encyclopedia of Folk Medicine* by Gabrielle Hatfield, published in 2004, carries instructions for the use of the oil to treat deafness. This remedy was of Romani origin and the oil was prepared by first baking the hedgehog whole in a clay covering. The encyclopaedia also records the use of hedgehog fat, mixed with bear's grease, to cure baldness. And referring to

A hedgehog and an adder in conflict is a common image. This image from an edition of the German magazine *Die Gartenlaube*, in 1878, shows that it was not just the ancient Egyptians who put store in the capacity of the hedgehog to resist the snake.

William Salmon's publication of 1693, *Seplasium*: *The Compleat English Physician*, Hatfield introduces us to the idea of hedgehog dung also being a hair restorative. Additional variations suggest that mixing hedgehog oil with rosemary and nettle is particularly efficacious.

Kidney stones, too, could be dealt with thanks to the hedgehog, though in the eighteenth-century remedy reported by Andrew Allen in *A Dictionary of Sussex Folk Medicine*, it is the hedgehog skin, complete with prickles, that needs to be roasted, powdered and then added to a drink. Were these remedies rediscoveries or did the ideas travel with people as they moved around the world? The ancient Egyptians were also reputed to eat hedgehogs, cooked in the manner more famously associated with Romani people: baked in clay.[3]

The Chinese have a long history of using wildlife in medicine, but there is a degree of confusion as to whether or not the hedgehog plays a role in Traditional Chinese Medicine (TCM). There are some practitioners who are adamant that there is no place for the hedgehog in the diverse lists of remedies, but there are other documents that suggest that at least some people think they should be used. Hedgehog skin, for example, may be used to treat haemorrhoids; when roasted and ground into a fine powder and mixed with rice porridge it is said to be efficacious against diarrhoea; and for vomiting, the recommendation is to stir-fry the skin in sand, grind it to a powder, mix it with maize and ginger, then grind again and roll into round pills with honey.

When I visited China in search of the rarely seen *Hemiechinus hughi*, my attempts to track a hedgehog down lead me to Mr Liu Daming, who claimed to be breeding the animals for TCM. His website described a veritable menagerie of centipedes,

Liu Daming from Chuzhou, Anhui province, eastern China, breeds a number of animals for Chinese Traditional Medicine. This is a Daurian hedgehog, *Hemiechinus dauricus,* that was soon after purchased by the author and subsequently released back into the wild.

scorpions, leeches, flour beetles and hedgehogs. The enterprise was just outside Chuzhou, Anhui province, and it was rather less well appointed than the website implied. Daming had just one hedgehog, probably *H. dauricus* (Daurian hedgehog), a red-tailed centipede and a few beetles.

It seems that while the 'traditional' TCM does not involve hedgehogs, there are many folk remedies that have become incorporated along the way, resulting in their inappropriate appropriation by healers and salesmen.

The Chinese are not alone in looking to the hedgehog for a cure for ailments. In a review from 1962 of the Roma medical folklore of Hungary, many uses are considered:

It is interesting to note that some animals play a great role in Gypsy medical treatment. In Kérsemlyén the bristles of the hedgehog (*Erinaceus europaeus* L.) are cut and burned; the smoke is inhaled by a Gypsy having a cold. In Mátészalka, the Hungarian Gypsies heal wounds by putting the ashes of the burned bristles on them. Hedgehog grease is often smeared on parts of the body afflicted by rheumatism. Sometimes the afflicted area is smeared with the urine of a hedgehog, or with the grease of a gopher (*Spermophilus citeleus* L.). It is believed in Panyola that only the rendered grease of a hedgehog caught before St George's Day, 24 April, is useful.[4]

The healing properties of the hedgehog are not restricted to the physical, however. They have a long history of being used to treat spiritual ailments, as well.

SACRED HEDGEHOGS

Stonehenge has revealed a long-held fascination with the hedgehog. During an excavation in 2008, along the west side of the monument, archaeologists uncovered the skeleton of a three-year-old child from the British Late Bronze Age, around 3,000 years ago (*c.* 1000–700 BC). Associated with the remains was a small chalk carving of an animal, found in such a position as to suggest it might have been in the child's hand when buried.

The immediate reaction from the team was that this was a hedgehog, and while there is now some debate as to what species of animal it represents, it is appealing to think that the hedgehog might have been there as a favourite toy, given to accompany the child in the afterlife; or that the hedgehog, being nocturnal, could be a guide in the dark; or, given its talent for hibernation, might imbue the body with the capacity of revivification. The discovery raises the questions of how significant hedgehogs were in Bronze Age Britain, and whether they were associated with any form of worship. This is the only carving of an animate creature found at Stonehenge so far.

The ancient Greeks considered the hedgehog a representative of Artemis, the goddess of the hunt. There is a beautiful alabaster hedgehog dedicated to the goddess in the Archaeological Museum of Brauron in Attica dated to around 600 BC. Also linked to Artemis was the practice in southern Tyrol, Austria, of taking spiky balls made of wood and painted red – known as *Stachelkugeln* – into places of worship and to graves. These ex-voto offerings were based on the form of a cow's uterus following calving, which is known in the region as *igelkalb*, or 'hedgehog's calf'. Dating back to the fifth millennium BC there is 'archaeological evidence [that] shows the Great Goddess' epiphany in the form of a hedgehog'.[5]

China has been the home of some of the most overt reverence given to the hedgehog. In 1948 Li Wei-tsu outlined his anthropological research in his paper 'On the Cult of the Four Sacred Animals (*Szu Ta Men*) in the Neighbourhood of Peking'. The beliefs he describes marry ancient shamanic and folk traditions with Taoism. The four sacred animals were the fox, weasel, hedgehog and snake. He found that there was a great deal of importance attached to being able to identify which of the individual members of each species are 'sacred' – possessing higher, supernatural qualities – and which are 'profane' and may be hunted.

Collecting the wisdom of the people living on the land, Wei-tsu was able to piece together the key elements of the local beliefs. In the *pai-men* – the hedgehog family – it is possible to identify a profane individual because it

> simply displays the ordinary grey colour of its spines and does not show any outstanding peculiarity whatsoever. A sacred hedgehog is characterized by its red eyes and white hair of about one inch on its chest. The tip of each bristle on the other parts of its body resembles a pearl. The colour of the sacred hedgehog is inconstant, at one time it is white, at another grey or black. In strolling around it does not show the timidity usual with hedgehogs during daytime.

This would suggest that albino hedgehogs were considered sacred, as they are the only ones with red eyes, but that characteristic is, obviously, restricted to those animals that are all-white. And the behaviour of strolling around in the daytime would suggest a sick hedgehog. Rather fascinatingly, the propensity for the hedgehog to become roadkill is woven into the mythology. A hedgehog may quest magical self-perfection on its way to becoming a sacred individual, but along the way may encounter its own end:

> When a certain stage on the way to perfection is reached, the hedgehog will be compelled by its own soul-power (*ling-hsing*) to lay itself down on the road in the tracks of vehicles out of longing for being crushed by the wheels.

These animals are important to have around: of the four sacred creatures, the hedgehog is considered to be the pre-eminent bringer of wealth. Li tells of how the animals are accommodated: places where hedgehogs are known to reside are not to be disturbed; a wheat-straw pile is referred to as a 'gold thread apartment' on account of its valuable inhabitants.

Failure to treat hedgehogs with due respect could have troubling consequences for the people involved. Li relates the tale of an eleven-year-old girl who was struck with a serious illness; it was identified by a shaman as being caused by the spirit of a hedgehog from a family of hedgehogs that had been killed by the girl's brother. It seems that perhaps it would have been more appropriate if her brother had been the one reduced to violent stomach cramps. Sometimes the hedgehogs would exhibit leniency. The story of a small boy who buried two hedgehogs alive for fun could have had a horrible ending. Luckily, his mother dug them up in a hurry and prayed forgiveness, and so 'The *Pai-yeh* went back to their former shelter and did not take possession of other people.' Indeed, according to local Chinese belief, sacred hedgehogs could themselves develop sensitivities to their human neighbours, to the point of picking up their own religious principles:

> The hedgehog spirit of the magician Li also claimed to be a Mohammedan. The offerings made to him by the family of the magician were only vegetables and eggs. Pork was tabooed. One day another native dressed pork in his own room. During his work the stove as well as the cooking vessel fell to the ground, breaking to pieces without any visible reason, and the ground was stained with gravy. The man was greatly astonished and told this incident to magician Li. From her he learned that the

hedgehog had been offended by the existence of pork in the house.[6]

The spines of the hedgehog have featured as one of five amulets carried by the Mongols of the Ordos Desert as a charm against evil spirits. The hedgehog was also crucial for protection against the dragon Dzalmaus Peigambar. The myth goes that the dragon was devouring cattle and people in the region. A hedgehog, Kerpek Sheshen, tricked the dragon into swallowing him, whereby his spines created enough discomfort to persuade the dragon to consider forgoing his devouring of livestock and humans. It was then agreed that on the presentation of gold the dragon would desist, and the hedgehog was released from the dragon's stomach. But where to find the gold?

> On the road there met him a man all in white, his head also was bound with a white fillet. The white man asked Kerpek Sheshen where he was going. The hedgehog informed him. Then the white man (he was Musa Peigambar, the prophet Moses) led him to a great water, and dug into it with his staff, and broke out a lump of gold like a horse's head. Kerpek Sheshen took the gold to Dzalmaus; and then he ceased to eat people.[7]

While today we may consider the hedgehog benign and occasionally a little dim – a safe and unthreatening animal, hardly one to be defeating a great dragon like Dzalmaus – there have been other grand versions of this bundle of spines, again resting on the animal's perceived wisdom. For example, Eastern European myths and legends accorded hedgehogs enormous respect, even to the extent of their being considered superior to a supposedly omniscient God.

One Romanian creation myth has the hedgehog, albeit inadvertently, ensuring that life can flourish on the newly formed earth. When God had completed making the world, He found that, due to His enthusiasm, He had spread the land out so far that there was no room for water. And this left nowhere for the fish. In desperation He sent a bee as a messenger to consult the wisest of creatures, the hedgehog. This hedgehog was not of the benign kind, and responded, 'Go away! God knows everything and please stop bothering me.' But the bee persisted, and remembered that the hedgehog frequently talked to himself. So, waiting in the bushes for some mumbled wisdom, the bee heard the hedgehog say, 'God does not know that he needs valleys and mountains in order to make room for the water. He must pick up the earth's skirts and create them.' And with this message the bee returned to God, and we now have a world diverse in its valleys and flourishing, for the time being, with fish.[8]

THE SOURCE OF MANY MYTHS

Many of today's myths surrounding the hedgehog were initially purported as fact. The progenitor of numerous myths was Pliny the Elder and the following, from his *Natural History* written in around AD 77, develops ideas that themselves came from Aristotle; not all of them are factually accurate.

Hedgehogs also lay up food for the winter; rolling them-selves on apples as they lie on the ground, they pierce one with their quills, and then take up another in the mouth, and so carry them into the hollows of trees . . . when they conceal themselves in their holes, afford a sure sign that the wind is about to change from north-east to south. When they perceive the approach of the hunter, they draw in the head and feet, and all the lower part of the body, which is covered by a thin and defenceless down only, and then roll themselves up into the form of a ball, so that there is no way of taking hold of them but by their quills. When they are reduced to a state of desperation, they discharge a corrosive urine, which injures their skin and quills, as they are aware that it is for the sake of them that they are hunted . . .

[Hunters] force it to unroll itself, by sprinkling warm water upon it, and then, suspended by one of its hind legs, it is left to die of hunger; for there is no other mode of destroying it, without doing injury to its skin . . . If it were not for the quills which it produces, the soft fleece of the sheep would have been given in vain to mankind; for it is by means of its skin, that our woollen cloth is dressed.[9]

The first description attracted the attention of illustrators of medieval bestiaries. The Aberdeen Bestiary contains one of the most famous of these images, while Isidore of Seville, writing in the seventh century, declared that the hedgehog will cut a bunch of grapes from a vine and roll over them so it can carry the grapes back to its young on its quills.[10] It is strange that the idea of hedgehogs carrying fruit on their spines lasted as long as it did, given that it is an animal that must have been seen with some regularity and this is something they simply do not do. In the first instance, they don't eat fruit, or at least not deliberately or with any regularity. At best, they will forage around fallen fruit in search of macro-invertebrate prey that will itself be feeding on it, so the hedgehogs are indirectly eating the fruit.

But how would the fruit get on to the back of the hedgehog? It has been suggested that fruit might become impaled as it falls from a tree. But this too is beset with difficulties. Ripe fruit falling on a relaxed hedgehog as it snuffles along an orchard floor will bounce off. The spines of a relaxed hedgehog are flat to its body. If a frightened hedgehog were to be stopped beneath a tree, there is a chance that a piece of fruit might become impaled, but as soon as the spines relax as it starts to walk, it would drop off. Additionally, hedgehogs do not take fruit back to their nests. The British hedgehog expert Pat Morris has examined hundreds of winter nests and has never found anything that could be construed as a larder.[11] This is to be expected: hedgehogs do not eat when hibernating but instead rely on the stores of fat laid down over the busy weeks of autumn as they feed on the invertebrates among the fallen and rotting fruit.

To test his observations, Morris declared to a BBC television audience of 12 million that the carrying of fruit on the spines of a hedgehog is a fiction; not one person responded by writing in to say they had seen it happen. That may not have been the most scientific of approaches, but it makes the point well.

Looking back to Pliny: his second point about the weather-predicting capacity of the hedgehog is dealt with a little later in this chapter. As to the corrosive discharge emanating from the frightened hedgehog, that is poppycock. It is worrying to consider how many hedgehogs might have suffered a death as prescribed by the learned Roman. The use of hedgehog skins to card wool is a real and genuine fact, however. Hedgehog skins were stretched over pieces of wood and then used to comb 'raw' wool, cleaning, separating and straightening the fibres before spinning. So important were hedgehog skins that rich merchants were accused of hoarding them in an

Hedgehogs collecting grapes, from the Aberdeen Bestiary, 12th century.

attempt to have their scarcity on the market increase their trade value.

The Bestiary of Albertus Magnus from the thirteenth century contains a delightful introduction to the animal. First there is the story of their wind-predicting capacity, but then comes this novel suggestion:

> It is an exception to all other four-legged beasts in having its genitals internally like a bird. For this reason it is often unchaste. It is also said that it has two anal holes, through which its waste matters pass, contrary to the nature of all other animals. The hedgehog mates in an upright position on account of the sharpness of its prickles.[12]

Again: behaviour that can never have been witnessed because it does not happen. And if people had started to measure legends against actual behaviour, an awful lot of misery and suffering on the part of hedgehogs could have been avoided. The authorities might have noticed that the declaration in 1566 of the hedgehog as vermin, with a bounty on its head of tuppence – the same as an otter and twice that of the more potentially deleterious pole-cat, stoat and weasel – was rather misplaced.

One of the crimes the hedgehog was alleged to commit was the theft of milk. It is easy to see how a hard-pressed milkmaid or herdsman with decreasing yields will scout around for a reason. Arriving at dawn and finding a recumbent cow, a small puddle of milk and a hedgehog with milky chops, it is

The Aberdeen Bestiary provides an image of fruit collecting hedgehogs that has inspired other artists, including Carol Mullin, who created this rich cushion cover.

Two hedgehogs, from the Northumberland Bestiary.

not difficult to jump to a conclusion. But it is also nonsense, and was frequently identified as such. In 1908 *The Times* carried a report from the Board of Agriculture stating that 'hedgehogs do not take the milk of cows that are lying down. The statement that they do so is . . . an old fallacy which was mentioned in the "New Catalogue of Vulgar Errors," published 120 years ago by Stephen Fovargue.' Fovargue's catalogue was published in 1767, at which time hedgehogs were still being hunted for a bounty; the error is defined: 'That the Hedge-Hog is a mischievous animal; and particularly, that he sucks cows, when they are asleep in the night, and causes their teats to be sore.' Fovargue's preface should, perhaps, be considered more often throughout the rest of his book: 'To explain the Use of Education, no Method can be more effectual, than to show what dull Mistakes and silly Notions Men are apt to be led into for Want of it.'

In Roger Lovegrove's brilliant yet disturbing book *Silent Fields* (2007), he reports the condemnation in 1829 of James Knapp, who described the hedgehog as this most harmless and least obtrusive creature . . . yet [they] give rewards for the wretched urchin's head [because of] that very ancient prejudice of its drawing milk from the udders of resting cows being still entertained without any consideration of its impracticability from the smallness of the Hedgehog's mouth.[13]

Knapp was not alone in identifying this considerable flaw, as evidenced by the nineteenth-century poet John Clare's 'The Hedgehog':

> They say they milk the cows and when they lye
> Nibble their fleshy teats and make them dry
> But they whove seen the small head like a hog
> Rolled up to meet the savage of a dog
> With mouth scarce big enough to hold a straw
> Will neer believe what no one ever saw
> But still they hunt the hedges all about
> And shepherd dogs are trained to hunt them out
> They hurl with savage force the stick and stone
> And no one cares and still the strife goes on[14]

Lovegrove pored over the parish records that recorded the payment of bounties for all sorts of slaughter and found that in the ten British counties for which he had the most data, around half a million hedgehogs were killed between 1660 and 1800. Conservatively scaling this up gives a figure of at least 2 million hedgehogs killed for bounty in 140 years.

Though that sounds devastating, it should be compared to estimates today of the numbers of hedgehogs killed on the roads; in Britain the low estimate is of 15,000 hedgehogs killed each year, though there are far higher figures suggested. Still, this is roughly the same as the quantities deliberately slaughtered for bounty in previous centuries: around 14,000 per year, based on extrapolating from Lovegrove's work.

The suggestion has been made that the error in selecting the hedgehog for a cull was deliberate, that it might in fact have been a form of social security, indicating to poor people that they could get a small amount of money for simple yet useless work and at the same time, as only the head had to be presented, get a meal into the bargain.[15]

Of course, there was much more to the hedgehog than being labelled as a milk and egg thief. And while it seems to have been very much a 'folk' animal, there is plenty of evidence that it was an important one. When we turn to the literature that has been generated in the name of the hedgehog, we will see this clearly.

BIBLES AND FAIRY TALES

The low opinion some had for the hedgehog might have been informed by its place in the Bible. Or rather, in some Bibles; there is an amusing inconsistency in translations, which demonstrate confusion of animals as different as a hedgehog and a bittern. Consider Isaiah 34:11 across two standard translations:

But pelican and hedgehog will possess it, And owl and raven will dwell in it; And He will stretch over it the line of desolation And the plumb line of emptiness. (*New American Standard Bible*)

But the cormorant and the bittern shall possess it; the owl also and the raven shall dwell in it: and he shall stretch out upon it the line of confusion, and the stones of emptiness. (*King James Bible*)

This bas-relief on the cathedral in Amiens, northern France, is a representation from the biblical story of the destruction of Nineveh.

Another appearance of the hedgehog in the Bible refers to its presence in the ruins of Ninevah (Zephaniah 2:14), but again it depends on which translation you refer to whether it is a spiny mammal or a heron-like bird. The Ninevah story has been represented as a bas-relief on the facade of Amiens Cathedral in France. Perhaps the absence of other representations featuring the heron is evidence for the primacy of the hedgehog version.

The reference in this is clearly not positive – an area ravaged by a vengeful God being described as fit for hedgehogs. It is a very different picture to the one we have today of a benign or even beneficent animal. Hedgehogs therefore provided material for earlier sermonizers, with one of the most famous comparing sinners to hedgehogs. In his book of medieval preachers and medieval preaching, John Mason Neale presented the preaching of St Anthony of Padua (1195–1231).[16] In the sermon of the Second Sunday in Lent the saint explains Isaiah's thoughts about the hedgehog:

NOTE that the hedgehog is altogether full of prickles; and if any one tries to take it, it rolls itself up, and becomes as it were a ball in the hand of the holder. Its head and its mouth are set low down, and inside its mouth are five teeth. The hedgehog is the obstinate sinner, covered all over with the prickles of sins. If you endeavour to convince him of the sin he has committed, he immediately rolls himself up, and hides, by excusing, his fault. And thus it may be said that his head and mouth are set low down. By the head, we understand, the thoughts; by the mouth, the words. While the sinner excuses himself with respect to the sin he has done, what else is it than that he bows his mind and his words down to the ground? Whence also he is said to have five teeth in his mouth, which are the five kinds of excuses that are found in the mouth of the obstinate. For, when he is blamed, he excuses himself either by ignorance or chance, or the suggestion of the devil, or the frailty of his flesh, or the occasion given by his neighbour.

There is much that both the hedgehog lover and the naturalist would find to fault in this thesis, not least the idea that the hedgehog possesses only five teeth. But not every religious reference to the hedgehog was so unpleasant. In fact the hedgehog can be said to have quite a supporting role, at least in the chapel of New College, Oxford, founded at the end of the fourteenth century, where two of the animals appear, carved in wood, supporting one of the misericords – though whether the central female centaur with an axe is a threat to the hedgehogs is not clear. It is also interesting that both hedgehogs have two items of fruit attached to their spines, again reiterating that myth.

Many of the misericords have very pagan images; Green Men and strange animals abound, often surrounded by delicate leaves. The hedgehogs providing mercy in Cartmel priory, Cumbria, share the space with similar pagan images. A further fifteenth-century misericord featuring a hedgehog can be found in the Cathedral of Saint Jean de Maurienne in Savoie, France.

Hedgehogs have, unsurprisingly, found their way into folk tales throughout the world. Again, it is not in the grand narrative that they are most comfortable but in the stories closer to the ground. There is a series of stories from Africa featuring the relationship between a hedgehog and either a jackal or a dog; there is a theme running through them, of the jackal believing it has outwitted the hedgehog and the hedgehog recovering with often fatal consequences for the deceitful jackal.

Some of the best collections of folk tales come from the poet and novelist Andrew Lang. Working at the turn of the twentieth century, he found several other stories that link the jackal and the hedgehog, though given the outcomes, the beginning is a little misleading:

> In a country which is full of wild beasts or all sorts there once lived a jackal and a hedgehog, and, unlike though they were, the two animals made great friends, and were often seen in each other's company.

What happens is in many ways similar to the ancient Greek poet Archilochus' adage 'The fox knows many things, but the hedgehog knows one big thing.' It would be wonderful to know if the publication by Lang in 1906 was influenced by Archilochus, or whether these tales from Africa are ancient enough to have found their way into the Greek canon or whether, like convergent evolution, the idea emerged in more than one place

Again caught in the mythological act of carrying away fruit, these hedgehogs were carved into a misericord at New College, Oxford, in the 14th century. The centaur remains a mystery.

Hedgehog in the margin of the Luttrell Psalter, 14th century.

independently. Perhaps the folk tales influenced Isaiah Berlin too, because as we shall see later, he was very taken by these two animals as a metaphor, which has now run and run.

One of the tales in Lang's collection, 'The Adventures of a Jackal', begins with the two protagonists stealing corn. Deceit and mischief follow, resulting in an act of revenge by a shepherd who presents them with a sheep that is actually a greyhound in disguise. It is the hedgehog, 'who sometimes showed more cunning than anyone would have guessed', who sees through the disguise and runs away. The jackal likes to consider himself the wisest of the wise, and is inevitably eaten. Later still, the eldest son of the jackal encounters the hedgehog and attempts to cheat him. The hedgehog is wise, though, and tells the jackal that many people are coming so he should 'Lie down here, and I will throw these sacks over you. And keep still for

58

ra uitam meam ꝛ gloꝛiam meam
in puluerem deducat

Exsurge domine in ira tua: ꝛ exalta
re in finibus inimicoꝛum meoꝛū.

Et exsurge domine deus meus in
precepto quod mandasti: ꝛ synago
ga populoꝛum circumdabit te.

Et propter hanc in altum regrede
re: dominus iudicat populos.

Iudica me domine secundum iusti
ciam meam: et secundum innocen
ciam meam super me

Consumetur nequicia peccatoꝛum
et diriges iustum: scrutans coꝛda

your life, whatever happens.' What follows is a little out of character for hedgehogs in modern literature: 'the hedgehog set a great stone rolling, which crushed him to death.'

Very similar traditional stories are found in Romania, Russia and Greece. Sometimes the relationship between the hedgehog and the fox in these tales is mutual and positive. Sometimes the endings are surprising. But they all revolve around the theme of the fox having many wits (and boasting about them) and the hedgehog admitting to being very simple.

The Romanian tale is titled 'The Fox and His Bagful of Wits and the One-witted Hedgehog'. Here the fox persuades the hedgehog to come and join it in a raid on a poultry farm. But the farmers are ready and have laid a pit trap, into which the protagonists fall. Having declared his great wit and intelligence, the fox is asked for a solution to their plight. When none is forthcoming, the hedgehog declares that the fall has made him feel sick. The fox, keen not to have his misery compounded by a pit filled with vomit, grabs hold of the hedgehog and throws him out. Chuckling to the fox, the hedgehog says, 'Where is your wisdom, you fool? You boast that you have a bagful of wits, whilst it is I who get myself out of the pit, though I have only a little wit.' But this is a merciful hedgehog who responds to the entreaties of the trapped fox.

> 'Well', said the hedgehog, 'I will help you. Now, you pretend to be dead, and when the people come and find you stiff and stark, and a nasty smell about you, they will say, "The fox has died, and his carcass is rotting. It is going to make all the poultry yard offensive." They will take you and throw you out. And then see whither your way lies.'[17]

From the same collection, *Rumanian Bird and Beast Stories* (1915), comes a tale with a similar trap but a different outcome. The hedgehog and the boastful fox were in a hole.

The hedgehog said, 'I have only three wits. Perhaps you will save me first, then I will see about you afterwards', and he asked the fox to pitch him out of the hole.

The fox did so, and then asked the hedgehog whether he could help him.

The hedgehog said, 'I cannot help you with three, if you cannot help yourself with seventy-seven.'

And so the fox was caught in the morning by the peasants and killed.

The Greek version, however, reveals an interesting twist. This time the trap is made of iron and the fox is caught:

She called out, 'Help me, Hedgehog! I'm caught in a trap.'

He said, 'Empty the tricks out of your bag, so I can free you.'

The fox said, 'I jumped over a ditch, and all my tricks fell out. Don't you know even one?'

The hedgehog replied, 'I know two of them. The one is that when the farmer comes, just play dead; the other is that while you are playing dead you should let a mighty fart.'

This works wonderfully and the fox escapes. But later the hedgehog becomes trapped.

He called out, 'Help me, Mistress Fox, I'm caught in a trap. Empty out your tricks and free me from the trap.'

The fox replied, 'I jumped over a ditch again, and all my tricks fell out.'

The hedgehog family is celebrating their victory over the arrogant hare with the gold coin and a bottle of brandy from the story collected by the Brothers Grimm. This illustration, probably by Carl Offterdinger, is from a late 19th-century book of fairy tales.

The hedgehog said, 'Since I am about to die, forgive me of my sins.'

The fox said, 'If you will forgive me all of my sins against you, then I will ask God to forgive you of all your sins.'

Then the hedgehog asked, 'Come closer and we'll hug one another, because we have lived together for such a long time.'

The fox went to him, and they hugged one another. Then the hedgehog said, 'You should also kiss me on the mouth.'

The fox did so, but the hedgehog grabbed hold of her tongue with his teeth and held her there until the farmer came by. When the farmer saw how the hedgehog had caught the fox he laughed, then he killed the fox and let the hedgehog run away.[18]

The cunning and wisdom of the hedgehog was picked up by the Brothers Grimm. In their moral tale 'The Hare and the Hedgehog' the hedgehog challenges the arrogant hare to a race, with a bottle of brandy and a gold coin – a louis d'or – being the wager. The hedgehog's wife is not impressed, questioning his sanity. But she comes with him at his request and assists in the challenge. As the race begins, the hare sprints like the wind and the hedgehog hides, only for his wife to appear at the finishing line. The race is repeated 73 times, and every race has the same outcome. On the 74th occasion the hare drops down dead, killed by his arrogance.

The essence of the tale also appears in an English version featuring the Devil in the role of the hare. 'This went on . . . until they ran the Devil to death.'[19] And a version featuring a stag as the arrogant challenger does not have such a dramatic conclusion, though the winner, by the same strategy, remains the same.[20]

MODERN MYTHOLOGY

When does folklore become real? How many times has a story to be told, however fictitious it may be, to attract a veneer of acceptability? It is possible that future generations will really consider that the American celebration of Groundhog Day comes directly from an ancient ritual known as Hedgehog Day. Each year on the second day of February, at Gobbler's Knob just outside Punxsutawney in Pennsylvania, a groundhog (a type of marmot) called Phil is called upon to predict the weather. If the weather is cloudy, and Phil casts no shadow, it is decided that winter will soon end, but if there is sunshine and a shadow, well, winter will last another six weeks. His success rate is somewhat below chance, at 39 per cent, according to the website of the Stormfax Weather Almanac.

The origins of Groundhog Day come from the pagan festival Imbolc (or St Brighid's Day), via the Christian celebration of Candlemas, which gives rise to this educational ditty:

> If Candlemas be fair and bright
> Come, winter, have another flight.
> If Candlemas brings clouds and rain,
> Go, winter, and come not again.

Groundhog Day has become quite a festival, made more famous by the very clever film of the same name, released in 1993. But the community of pet-hedgehog keepers in the United States, in their desire for validation, have done a very good job at creating new mythologies in support of their obsession with keeping hedgehogs as pets. Their story goes that there was once an ancient Roman festival called Hedgehog Day, where the shadow of a hedgehog would be the predictor of an extended winter. The idea is that the Romans passed this ritual on to the Germanic tribes, where it lurked, emerging on the arrival of these people in the New World where, failing to find a hedgehog, they plumped for a groundhog instead.

So deeply set is this idea that hedgehog fans across the u.s. have taken 2 February to be a day of such significance that plans are made to ensure that weddings and other important events coincide with it, which is why it is a shame that the story has no grounding in truth at all: there was no Hedgehog Day in ancient Rome. However, there are weather-related traditions in Europe featuring, for example, the badger or the bear. Both these animals in European myth filled the role that was adopted by the groundhog in the U.S. And Pliny the Elder also imbued the hedgehog with weather-prophesying capabilities. Embellishing the work of Aristotle, he imagined that hedgehogs could tell you the weather by the careful observation of which of the two entrances to its burrow was blocked up. Unfortunately hedgehogs don't make burrows, though they will borrow burrows from other animals such as rabbits when the opportunity arises.

'Made up' folklore is delightfully seductive and as such can lead one to hope it was based on more than wishful thinking, not least the stories of the pixies of Devon and Cornwall who shape-shift into hedgehog form. Could it be that the origins of the word 'pixie' come from 'pig' – or 'hedgepig' – which were in part so named because of their flesh when cooked was considered similar to pork?

EATING HEDGEHOGS

Throughout the historical record there are references to the consumption of hedgehogs by humans. The fact, as mentioned above, that Roma and other travelling people would eat hedgehogs wrapped in clay and baked has been accorded folk-tale status; indeed, it is a folk tale that benefits from being true.

'Clay baking is the most effective way of cooking hedgehogs and small birds', explains the experimental archaeologist Jacqui Wood. She adds, 'You do not have to bother with the spines or feathers. When baked they come away from the flesh beautifully . . . and they do taste like pork, hence the hog in the name.' An early, somewhat gruesome, recipe comes from 'An Account of the Moorish Way of Dressing Their Meat', which was published in the Royal Society's *Philosophical Transactions* of 1699:

The Hedgehog is a Princely Dish among them, and before they kill him, rub his Back against the Ground, by holding its Feet betwixt two, as Men do a Saw that saws Stones, till it has done squeaking; then they cut its Throat, and with a Knife cut off all its Spines and singe it. They take out its Guts, stuff the Body with some Rice, sweet Herbs, Garavancas, Spice, and Onions; they put some Butter and Garavancas into the Water they stew it in, and let it stew in a little Pot, close stopped, till it is enough, and it proves an excellent Dish.

'Garavancas' may be related to garbanzo beans, better known as chickpeas.

The accounts of cooking hedgehog in Britain spring mainly from its travelling people, though others too have had a try. As a student, former TV personality and environmentalist Professor David Bellamy ate one stuffed with herbs. And there has been plenty of attention paid to Arthur Boyt, from Cornwall, who described in a BBC interview how he lived on nothing more than his home-grown vegetables and roadkill. He even gave a recipe for 'hedgehog spaghetti carbonara' to *The Guardian*.[21]

Over the millennia, hedgehogs have sustained us both physically and spiritually. From defence against the dark forces of the supernatural, through cures to most maladies and on to being a metaphor for a less boastful life, they persist with a vigour matched by few other wild animals.

3 Historical Hedgehogs

The experience of the hedgehog in the chronicles of natural history has already been hinted at. Some early comments regarding their dietary and mating preferences were clearly wide of the mark. Edward Topsell's *History of Four-footed Beasts*, published in 1607, is a wonderful merging of observation with the mythology laid down by the ancient Greeks and other fantastic tales. In his defence Topsell does make it clear that he is not a naturalist, and is only relating what is said by many others. Indeed, much of what he writes comes from the Swiss scholar Conrad Gesner's *Historiae animalium* (1551–8).

Topsell writes that when a fox approaches a hedgehog, rolled in a ball, he will

> licketh gently the face and snowt of the Hedgehogge, by that meanes bringing him to unfold himselfe againe, and to stand upon his legs, which being done, he instantly devoureth, or else poisoneth the beast with the urine that he rendereth upon the Hedgehogges face.

The story that foxes urinate on rolled-up hedgehogs to cause them to unfurl is long-standing and most likely untrue; a slight variation on the theme is that the fox will roll the hedgehog into water. Topsell's knowledge of the names of hedgehogs around Europe is of a remarkable range and indicates how wide his net of research must have been cast. The observations he describes are often very accurate. For example he writes about spines that 'are haire at the beginning, but afterwardes grow to be prickles', though he seems to be suggesting they have spines on their face and feet. While he observes that hedgehogs eat worms, he repeats the fallacy of their frugivorous nature along with their habit of collecting the fruit on their spines and storing it for the winter. Likewise he is confused about reproduction:

> When they are in carnall copulation they stand upright, and are not joyned like other beastes, for they imbrace one another, standing belly to belly: but the prickly thornes uppon their backes will not suffer them to have copulation like Dogges or Swine, and for this cause they are a very little while in copulation, because they cannot stand long together upon their hinder Legges.

In contrast, the description of a fight between a hedgehog and an adder is quite accurate, though they are far too anthropomorphized. It is unlikely that there is 'mortall hatred betwixt the Serpent and the Hedgehog' and when the hedgehog wins, there

The hedgehog in Conrad Gessner's *Historiae animalium* (1551).

By the 19th century illustrations were often superbly lifelike. This image is from *A History of British Quadrupeds* (1837) by Thomas Bell.

are probably more prosaic reasons behind the observation of the hedgehog 'carrying the flesh upon his speares, like an honorable banner won from his adversary in the field.' At least there is a reason why that action might have been seen. But it was surprising to read that there was

> also a story of hatred between the Hare and the hedghog, for it is said that a Hare was seene to plucke off the prickles from the Hedghog, and leave her bald, pieled, and naked, without any defence.

The differences between Topsell's work and the letters of the naturalist Gilbert White, published in his *The Natural History of Selborne* (1789), present a clear indication of the leaps taken by scholars in understanding the natural world. White discusses rearing a litter of young, describes the impact of the hedgehog on the garden as minimal and, though he mistakes grubbing in the ground for beetle larvae for consumption of the roots of plantain, he does observe their diet to be largely beetles, given the constitution of their dung.

This more scientific level of observation was becoming standard and by the time Georges-Louis Leclerc, Comte de Buffon, who has been described as 'the father of all thought in natural history',[1] published a 36-volume guide to natural history between 1749 and 1788, the amount of fancy and fallacy had been much reduced. Some of the descriptions are delightful: the hedgehog has 'the power of defending itself from an enemy without combating him, and of annoying without attacking him'. Still, in spite of the gains made in factual understanding, Buffon does go on to recount Pliny's myth of the repellent power of hedgehog urine.

Buffon gets their preferred natural habitat about right and declares, correctly, 'I do not believe that they climb up trees, as some naturalists have affirmed, or that they make use of their prickles to carry off the fruit.' It is perhaps a shame, then, that he goes on to spoil these observations by maintaining the fruit-diet falsehood, claiming 'it is with their mouth they seize it.' Back on the right track, Buffon critiques earlier writers with his observations of hibernation. 'They sleep during the winter; and therefore every thing that has been said of their laying up provisions for that season must be false.'

Contrary to modern thinking (which is at least in part motivated by the desire to discourage people from trying to tame wild European hedgehogs), Buffon states that 'The Hedgehog may be rendered domestic, and in that state is very useful in destroying cockroaches and beetles, which he pursues and devours with great activity. He is believed also to destroy mice nearly if not quite as well as a cat.' Another favourite of the animal's diet is revealed and helps explain the stubborn way it has remained in the mind of people to this day – he points out that the hedgehog will drop anything for a saucer of milk, though nowadays we know that despite their fondness for milk, it is not that good for them.

In 1766, Thomas Pennant's *British Zoology* was published by the Cymmrodorion society (which still promotes the language, arts and science of Wales today). This book contains one of the more disturbing descriptions of animal cruelty: 'The barbarity of the anatomists furnishes us with an amazing instance of [the hedgehog's] patience; one that was dissected alive, and whose feet were nailed down to the table; endured that, and every stroke of the operator's knife, without even one groan.'

At about the same time as Buffon was finishing his epic guide, Francis Fitzgerald was publishing his *Surveys of Nature, Historical, Moral, and Entertaining*. This again showed a considerable increase in understanding from earlier writing. There is a clear description of the animal along with an explanation of its absence during winter, during which time it does not eat. Still it is repeated that it eats fruit, but there is a delightful observation contained in the publication of 1787: 'On another occasion, a hedge-hog, that had made its way into the kitchen, discovered a little pot, in which was meat prepared for boiling; the mischievous animal drew out the meat, and left its excrements in the stead', a sight that will be familiar to anyone who has spent any time with a captive hedgehog.

Oliver Goldsmith's *An History of the Earth, and Animated Nature* (1774) draws much on Buffon, while Charles Knight's *Pictorial Half-Hours etc.* (1851) reads far more like more modern nature writing and gives some detail to the muscular adaptation the hedgehog has to enable it to roll into a ball. He clears the hedgehog of milk theft with barely concealed scorn and, while still

asserting that the hedgehog will eat fruit, dismisses the idea of
reserves being taken to a winter store on the animal's spines.
There is even a good description of a hibernaculum, giving this
an air of authority as a very accurate introduction to the species.

Throughout these natural histories much is made of the
unaggressive nature of the hedgehog; of how it is a defensive
creature. And these qualities were obviously going to inform
military minds as much as natural historians.

WARFARE

One of the earliest references to hedgehogs in warfare has the
spikes pointing the wrong way. In the *Oxford Dictionary of National
Biography* the entry for Ambroise, the chronicler of the Third
Crusade at the end of the twelfth century, refers to Richard I
returning 'from fighting on one occasion so covered with arrows
that *"il resembloit un heriçon"*' ('he looked like a hedgehog').

John June's engraving of a scene from the ballad 'The Dragon of Wantley', 1740s; the hedgehog-style knight, kicking a dragon in its fundament.

A more reasonable presentation of spikes was captured in the mid-eighteenth-century print of a scene from the ballad 'The Dragon of Wantley' held at the British Museum. A knight, 'More of More Hall', kicks a dragon in the backside. The knight is protected by a suit of armour that owes much to the hedgehog.

More offensively, at the Battle of Bannockburn in 1314, Robert the Bruce trained his men to use a 'hedgehog' of spears against the onslaught of English heavy cavalry. An outward wall of pikes was called a hedgehog formation. Ranging in length from 3 m to 7.5 m, the wooden shaft and metal spearhead was an effective defensive weapon on the battlefield and was used extensively from the fourteenth to the eighteenth century. As guns became more common and effective, the hedgehog became rather less so.

But the name lingered on and was applied to anti-tank obstacles. Like giant caltrops, these angled lengths of iron were formed into patterns such that even when upset by a nearby explosion, they would remain effective. These defences formed part of the massive Czech–German border fortifications in the run up to the Second World War and have taken the name 'Czech hedgehogs'. They became very effective in urban conflict, where one 'hedgehog' could block an entire street. The technical specifications for an effective 'hedgehog' are that it should be able to withstand 60 tonnes of force and that it should be no more than 1.4 m high; the idea is not that it be an immovable obstacle, but that it is slightly larger than the clearance under a tank, so that attempts to ride through a 'hedgehog field' would result in the tank becoming stuck.

The hedgehog defence strategy employed in Britain was rather different. There, static anti-tank spikes in the water along the coast were referred to as 'admiralty scaffolding'. Hedgehog defence is not just about a spiky array of metal: it is also a tactic for defending against a blitzkrieg. The 'hedgehogs' are a series of

heavily fortified positions that can be defended from all sides. Attackers can move between the defences but each of the hedgehogs continues to fight, even when surrounded, thus keeping the invading troops busy.

Ironically, it was not a uniquely British idea, being used successfully by the Germans on the Eastern Front, as described in a letter to *The Times* on 5 June 1943:

> On 2 May the Red Army was said to have launched an attack on 'the German hedgehog city of Orel'. This novel use of the word means, I suppose, a city like the hedgehog when rolled into a ball, bristling all round with means of defence.

The 'Czech hedgehog'.

Resulting in less death, the hedgehog defence is also a pawn formation in chess. Originally a term referring to a cramped and defensive formation, it is now well recognized and has spawned its own literature: the Russian grandmaster Sergey Shipov's two-volume set is titled *The Complete Hedgehog*, and received rave reviews from the chess world.

From the land to the sea: a book published in 1666, *The Faithful Annalist, or the Epitome of English History*, is referred to in a letter to *The Times* of 1943:

> 'In 1530 one of the Kynge's Hedgehogs ankered by the Tower, caught fire and exploded killing an officer and seven men.' This was no doubt a floating powder hulk or ammunition vessel.
>
> Reading this makes me wonder if in this type of ship we have the clue to the vessels Drake set alight in Calais Roads nearly sixty years later on as they drifted down on the fleet ... known historically as the Spanish Armada. I have often thought it a smart piece of work to alter half a dozen ships in a few hours and set them blazing, and still floating, towards a definite goal, but if as is probable, these were naval hedgehogs, it is fairly simple ... What is most likely is that a squadron of hedgehogs joined Howard and Drake that day with supplies of shot, and six were utilised straight away without unloading their cargoes, and performed a timely and meritorious deed.

This is not the only naval hedgehog to be found. In fact, there have been four Royal Navy ships named after hedgehogs. The most recent HMS *Urchin* was launched on 8 March 1943 from Barrow. The HMS *Urchin* was first introduced in 1797, seeing action in Egypt in 1801 when the British expeditionary force ejected Napoleon's troops. The second incarnation was a Modified R Class destroyer launched in 1917; the third, a U Class submarine launched in 1940 and loaned to the Polish Navy, where it was renamed *Sokół*, or *Falcon*.[2] The 1943 incarnation of the *Urchin*, a U Class destroyer, saw battle in 1944 in the Mediterranean at Anzio, Italy, in Normandy and in the Adriatic before spending the rest of the war in the Pacific. HMS *Urchin*'s motto was wonderfully hedgehog-like: '*Armatus ad defendum*', Armed to Defend. And on the badge, the heraldic detail is described as, 'On a Field barry wavy of eight White and Blue a hedgehog Proper'.

'Urchin' badge.

Another heraldic hedgehog is to be found on the reverse of an oval, silver medal from 1647. The front of medal features a bust of Robert Kyrle, who commanded under Cromwell as a captain of troopers. But the real interest lies with the hedgehogs. The armorial shield is garnished with the Abrahall crest, featuring three hedgehogs. The Abrahall family came from Herefordshire

Edwin Landseer, *Jocko with a Hedgehog*, 1828, oil on canvas.

Oval silver medal from 1647 featuring a bust of Robert Kyrle on one side and his armorial shield on the other. Top right of the shield are the three hedgehogs of the Abrahall crest.

and had as their motto, 'He who touches me, beware or repent.' There is also another hedgehog sat atop the shield. There is good reason for the association with the hedgehog; the Southern Marches were referred to by the Celts as 'Ergyng' – the land of the hedgehogs. The area of southern and western Herefordshire became known as Archenfield – clearly related to the old name for hedgehog, 'urchin'. The memory of this can be seen in the Abrahalls cider produced by Celtic Marches, which features a hedgehog on the label.

Mostly, though, the hedgehog is not considered a martial beast. Though 'armed to defend', it is also one of our most endearing and loved species, one that has inveigled its way into the hearts of many, and from there into stories, art and advertising.

Embracing the hedgehog motif, Celtic Marches have developed a cider that has used the Abrahall signature species.

4 Literary Hedgehogs

As over time our understanding of the hedgehog, and conse-
quently the writings of its natural history, has changed, so have
the ways in which the hedgehog has appeared in literature. We
have been seen already how folk tale and biblical references
equate the hedgehog with either desolation or craftiness.

It seems likely that Shakespeare was inspired by the Celtic
word for hedgehog, *grainneog*, which translates as 'the horrible
one', when he cast it among other low beasts in *A Midsummer
Night's Dream* (Act II, Scene 3):

> You spotted snakes with double tongue,
> Thorny hedgehogs, be not seen;
> Newts and blindworms, do no wrong,
> Come not near our fairy Queen.

And in *Richard III*, Act I, Scene 2, Lady Anne abuses Gloucester,
soon to be the eponymous king, by calling him a hedgehog, linking the appearance of the hedgehog, and the Celtic horribleness
associated with its name, to Gloucester's misshapen form.

> Dost grant me, hedgehog? then, God grant me too
> Thou mayst be damned for that wicked deed!
> O, he was gentle, mild and virtuous!

The stories associating hedgehogs with portent and doom continued. For example, a folk tale collected from Scotland in 1889 told how a meeting with a hedgehog on a bridge was considered an omen of disaster. Soon after the event a young girl fell into the river and drowned, some distance from the bridge on which she had met the animal. Locals were unwavering in their belief that her sighting of the hedgehog on the bridge must have been at the heart of the disaster.[1]

TRANSFORMATIONS

If it was not portent then it was magical transformation. Perhaps the most famous of the transformative hedgehogs comes in many versions, some far darker than others, but the essence remains the same. 'Hans My Hedgehog', in the version from the Brothers Grimm, starts with a man and his wife who are desperate for a child. The man is teased for his lack of offspring, and

> At last he became angry, and when he got home he said, 'I will have a child, even if it be a hedgehog.' Then his wife had a child that was a hedgehog in the upper part of his body and a boy in the lower.'

Despite eight years of benign neglect, the hedgehog, christened Hans, survived, and was presented on request with bagpipes and a shod cock. He left for the forest where he made beautiful music and twice guided lost kings to safety on the understanding that they would give to Hans the first thing they met on their return. In both instances it was their daughter. When Hans came to collect on his debt the first king was duplicitous and tried to have him killed. But Hans ended up taking away the daughter and exhibiting behaviour that might be shocking for present-day storybook readers:

> Hans the Hedgehog took her pretty clothes off, and pierced her with his hedgehog's spikes until she bled all over. 'That is the reward of your falseness,' said he. 'Go your way, I will not have you!' and on that he chased her home again, and she was disgraced for the rest of her life.

The second king honoured his promise and, though terrified, his daughter consented. But on that first night the hedgehog asked his new wife to wait until he had fallen asleep and, once he was, to throw his spiny skin, which he took off to go to bed, into the fierce fire. This she did, leaving him blackened but completely human. There was a beauty in the beast after all.[2]

A hundred years later and there were still hedgehog transformation stories. Edith Nesbit incorporated transformation magic into the brilliant tale of 'The Princess and the Hedgehog' (1974). And the beautifully illustrated *Princess Kalina and the Hedgehog* by Jeannette Flot, adapted by Frances Marshall and published in 1981, has as its conclusion a similar transformation. This time the love of a princess unwittingly rescues the enchanted Prince Porkio from his hedgehog state. It even ends the way all fairy tales should end: 'So they were married, had a great many children and lived happily ever after.'

Another transformation comes from the story of Aldegonda, collected from Florence in 1893. This fairy of the country was found in a mass of ivy by a peasant who was led there by a hedgehog. The peasant returned with both and asked his wife to treat them with kindness. But she already had a daughter, and as her daughter grew more ugly, so Aldegonda grew more beautiful. Jealous, the daughter of the peasant reacted by killing

Perhaps the most famous game of croquet ever played? Alice finds the use of hedgehogs and flamingos make it 'a very difficult game indeed'.

Mrs Tiggy-Winkle, from Beatrix Potter's *Tale of Mrs Tiggy-Winkle* (1905).

the hedgehog, who had become the fairy's friend, but in so doing she released the prince from the sorcerer's spell that would keep him a hedgehog until his lot combined to give him love and a violent death. This story ends with an incantation, 'Bestow, I pray, a favour! As with this leaf of ivy I make a sign of the cross, Which though wilt surely grant!', which leads the American folklorist Charles Godfrey Leland to consider it to be of a different heritage from the popular traditional tales from the Brothers Grimm, as it 'belongs to the dark lore current among witches and sorcerers, in which the story, although always ancient, is a mere frame for the ceremony and incantation.'[3]

Around the time that these tales with hints of menace were collected, hedgehogs appeared in a rather different guise: not lead characters, just parts of a game. And so it is to the most famous literary game of croquet in the world and Lewis Carroll's *Alice's Adventures in Wonderland* (1865).

> Alice thought she had never seen such a curious croquet-ground in her life: it was all ridges and furrows; the croquet balls were live hedgehogs, and the mallets live flamingoes, and the soldiers had to double themselves up and stand on their hands and feet, to make the arches.
>
> The chief difficulty Alice found at first was in managing her flamingo: she succeeded in getting its body tucked away comfortably enough under her arm, with its legs hanging down, but generally, just as she had got its neck nicely straightened out, and was going to give the hedgehog a blow with its head, it would twist itself round and look up in her face, with such a puzzled expression that she could not help bursting out laughing; and, when she had got its head down, and was going to begin again, it was very provoking to find that the hedgehog had unrolled itself, and was in the act of crawling away: besides all this, there was generally a ridge or a furrow in the way wherever she wanted to send the hedgehog to, and, as the doubled-up soldiers were always getting up and walking off to other parts of the ground, Alice soon came to the conclusion that it was a very difficult game indeed.[4]

For a number of years the people of Manitou Springs, Colorado, have celebrated Carroll's fantastical book with a festival that comes complete with a game of croquet, using the correct, if plastic, tools.

Our literary relationship with hedgehogs was about to take a great turn, away from playing the lead in dark tales to something altogether softer. Mrs Tiggy-Winkle has remained a favourite hedgehog since her first appearance in 1905. But her arrival on the scene was not a foregone conclusion. In his *Liaisons of Life: From Hornworts to Hippos* (2001), Tom Wakeford says that Beatrix Potter's story has 'become a legend of youthful scientific inquiry stifled by pomposity and prejudice'.[5] Indeed, Wakeford's insightful history of the once heretical science of symbiosis reveals a very different side to Potter's work.

Before committing herself to the entertainment of millions with her botanically accurate and beautifully illustrated children's books, Potter was a keen proponent of the idea of symbiosis, as manifest in lichen. She was one of a small group of scientists who countered popular belief and suggested that lichens were not a single organism but were in fact the result of a symbiotic relationship between algae and fungi. Her work was dismissed in part because of the way it confronted establishment beliefs, but mostly because she was a woman. It is noteworthy that the Linnean Society, after giving her a posthumous apology, held a meeting in her honour in 1997, 100 years after it had barred her from speaking.

The year of *The Tale of Mrs Tiggy-Winkle*'s publication also marked the point from which the hedgehog was almost entirely portrayed as positive. In the 1930s, Alison Uttley was writing about Fuzzypeg the Hedgehog with the key descriptors 'kindly' and 'simple'. The very peasant-like hedgehog in T. H. White's *The Once and Future King* (1939–41) is servile and simple. There was a dose of realism, heavily anthropomorphized, but still soundly rooted in some fact, in Phyllis Kelway's *Widow Hedgehog* (1934).

The most famous of the children's writers from the 1930s is Enid Blyton, and she tackled hedgehogs in very different ways. As part of her collection *Hedgerow Tales* she relates a relatively fact-based adventure, but in the more fantastical *The Careless Hedgehogs* there is an entire world of fairies and elves. The story concludes with the creation of the first protective chestnut skins out of these very unfortunate hedgehogs.

The next wave of hedgehog tales comes from the 1960s; Racey Helps published *Diggy Takes His Pick* in 1964 with Pinny Needlekin featuring as the slightly dim but kindly hedgehog. Molly Brett's *The Untidy Little Hedgehog* (1967) has similar characteristics. This is a by no means complete list of children's hedgehog stories, just a sprint through the snuffling mass. But there is a clear pattern developing. Hedgehogs were no longer being considered animals of doom and portent; they had now become almost exclusively a vehicle for wholesome and good-hearted, if occasionally simple, characters.

A wonderful spin on the older stories comes from Vivian French's *The Hedgehogs and the Big Bag* (1994). This time, four young hedgehogs outwit a fox in an easy-to-read romp. In fact, the early 1990s were a busy time for hedgehog stories, including the easiest of picture books, like the Percy the Park Keeper series by Nick Butterworth that has a hedgehog featuring as a leading, if, again, nice but dim, star.

It is fascinating how fairy tales are able to repeat fallacies and somehow get away with it. The story of hedgehogs collecting fruit on their spines was a staple, as we have seen, of the medieval bestiaries. And while it is demonstrably false, it reappears in the exquisitely illustrated *The Three Hedgehogs* by Javier Sáez Castán, which was published in 2003.

And still the hedgehog stories keep coming; especially so in a flourish of early reader chapter books, such as Dick King-Smith's

The Hodgeheg, published in 1987, and the *Animal Ark* series, which has two fairly accurate stories, 'Hedgehogs in the Hall' and 'Hedgehog Home'. Other early reader stories came in the form of 'Hedgehogs Don't Eat Hamburgers' by Vivien French and 'The Hedgehog's Prickly Problem' by Don Conroy.

Spikez, written by Richard Mayers and illustrated by John Burton – a new hero in hedgehog form – more fun than Sonic!

FOR THE OLDER READER . . .

Hedgehogs are well covered in early literature, but there has yet to be a fantasy as strong as *Watership Down* or *Duncton Wood* to catapult the animal into the same light as rabbits and moles (although there is a hedgehog in *Watership Down*, Yona is one of the mythical, and rather gossipy, characters). Or rather, there has not yet been a book that has quite captured the public's attention like that.

The Gathering: Secretly Saving the World (*Book One of the Hedgehog Chronicles*) by Z. G. Standing Bear manages to weave modern ecological concerns with Native American spirituality and use them to tell a tale of captive pet hedgehogs in the u.s. working together to save humanity from certain destruction. The *Quill Hedgehog* series by the Reverend Waddington-Feather consists of stories that again spring from the observation that 'progress' for people can be rather retrograde for everything else. And Phyllis Kidd self-published a long book called *The Urchins* in 1993 which seems to be a Christian allegory. But perhaps it will be down to Richard Mayer's *Spikez* (2012) to take the hedgehog to a new level. This robo-hog is armed and dangerous and determined to risk everything in defence of his home. It is rip-roaring entertainment and just might be the first real contender for a prickly breakthrough.

Not all literature has been fantasy-based; there is a strong tradition of trying to capture the natural history of the hedgehog through (occasionally anthropomorphic) writing. Unsurprisingly, Gerald Durrell had his moments with hedgehogs. As a boy in 1930s Corfu, as he relates in *Birds, Beasts, and Relatives*, he found a nest of four newborn hoglets.

> I visualized myself walking proudly through the olive groves, preceded by the dogs . . . and my two magpies and, trotting at my heels, four tame hedgehogs, all of which I would have taught to do tricks.

Unfortunately he did not have the expertise, and was also beset by a less than dutiful sibling who failed to follow instructions:

> They all died that night and Margo wept copiously over their balloon-like corpses. But her grief did not give me any pleasure . . . As a punishment to my over-indulgent sister, I dug four little graves and erected four little crosses in the garden as a permanent reminder, and for four days I did not speak to her.[6]

Caring for hedgehogs is tricky, as is the art of presenting an apparently fact-based insight into the real lives of hedgehogs. In G. D. Griffiths's *Mattie: The Story of a Hedgehog* (1967), there are many errors that, if taken as true, would threaten the welfare of any hedgehogs the reader might meet. Reflecting its time, the author has the hedgehogs dining on bread and milk, left as a supplement by kindly people. Now we know that, despite the avid consumption by hedgehogs, this is not a great food source. Hedgehogs are carnivores; they need the high protein and concentrated energy found in macro-invertebrates. Additionally, they do not digest milk very well and it can result in diarrhoea.

It is very sweet the way Griffiths has an attentive boar on hand to assist the pregnant female in the early stages of parenthood, but in actual fact the male's involvement ceases at ejaculation. But perhaps the most misleading comment comes when discussing a youngster:

> Although hedgehogs are now nocturnal animals, many thousands of years ago, when men were fewer and there were no vehicles, they hunted freely by day and by night. Even now, a young hedgehog is grateful for the warmth of the sun and loves to bask in it.[7]

There is no evidence that hedgehogs were ever diurnal, or indeed sleep-free, as this suggests. Hedgehog food is nocturnal; that is why hedgehogs occupy that niche, along with the added benefit of increased security by night. The only time a hedgehog will sunbathe is if it is ill. Usually this is related to hypothermia caused by lack of food, which is in turn caused by ill health.

One of the finest insights into the hedgehog, via narrative, was published in 1972. *Dearest Prickles, the Story of a Hedgehog Family* by Walter and Christl Poduschka manages to capture drama and fact in equal measure, charting the time the couple spend with a small family of hedgehogs. Benefiting greatly from being written by scientists, *Dearest Prickles* begins with a profound quote from the delightfully named German naturalist Johann Christian Polycarp Erxleben that in many ways captures perfectly the attraction the hedgehog has for many people.

> I have noticed that when people begin to make a special study of natural history, they all too often concentrate solely on foreign and rare specimens, believing that they already have sufficiently exact knowledge of the common

and indigenous ones. It should, however, be obvious that it is also extremely useful to become acquainted with just those very things which are native to one's own country.[8]

Following this advice, the Poduschkas catalogued their efforts to help four orphan baby hedgehogs found in their garden. Not shirking from their failings, they describe in detail the hard work required to keep them alive and the delight in seeing three make it through the winter. This book could have suffered from a surfeit of sentimentality had it been written by less scientific and aware authors. But Walter and Christl are very aware. Again near the beginning they make this clear, revealing something I am sure many similar enthusiasts have felt:

> Although many of our friends make kindly comments about our determined enthusiasm for hedgehogs, we secretly suspect them of thinking that our energies could be better employed elsewhere. Someone who occupies himself a great deal with animals and perhaps gives up some human contacts in consequence is considered – to put it mildly – abnormal or cranky. Anyone who is interested in animals and fond of them is well aware of this. This knowledge enables him to persist quite calmly in his crankiness, knowing that he will be understood perfectly by enthusiasts like himself.

The Poduschkas' story is translated from German and reminds us that, while there is a bias towards hedgehog stories in English, there are plenty of other people out there paying serious attention to the spiny mammal. For example, Pro Igel, the German hedgehog society, has collected books and articles about hedgehogs from around the world and now has a library with over

1,300 entries. And while the majority of these are technical and scientific papers, there is a substantial contribution in the form of children's books.

For an animal as readily recognizable and as unusual as the hedgehog there are surprisingly few references in the established canon of poetry; John Clare, whom we saw earlier, is a notable and predictable exception. Clare managed to capture life in a way so different to his classical allusion-obstructed contemporaries and was not afraid to enjoy and describe what he saw, a skill that makes his work all the more accessible to us today.

It is interesting that in the opening verse of his poem from the 1820s Clare repeats the fallacy of the hedgehog collecting fruit on its spines, but does so at one remove. Clearly he, a man of the hedgerow, had never witnessed this impossible gathering of food.

The Hedgehog

The hedgehog hides beneath the rotten hedge
And makes a great round nest of grass and sedge
Or in a bush or in a hollow tree
And many often stoops and say they see
Him roll and fill his prickles full of crabs
And creep away and where the magpie dabs
His wing at muddy dyke in aged root
He makes a nest and fills it full of fruit . . .

The only other person to have paid much attention to the hedgehog, and for it to have entered the canon (as I am sure there must have been a vast amount of folk poetry about the animal), was Charlotte Smith. Largely forgotten as a novelist, her poems from the late eighteenth century still persist. She had a tough life, realizing that, thanks to her useless husband, the only way to support her many children was for her to earn a living, which she did by writing:

The Hedgehog Seen in a Frequented Path

Wherefore should man or thoughtless boy
Thy quiet harmless life destroy,
Innoxious urchin? – for thy food
Is but the beetle and the fly,
And all thy harmless luxury
The swarming insects of the wood.

Smith clearly views the hedgehog with the same sort of kindly eye as other storytellers. But what would the most visceral of poets make of the animal? Scouring the collected works of Ted Hughes, I was startled to find not a single reference. It was only when wallowing in his letters that I found how deeply he felt for this wonderful animal. He recounts how he carried home a hedgehog, thinking it might make a good companion for the night, only to find that the confinement distressed the animal: 'I could have kissed him for compassion', he said, concluding that he is, and quite rightly so, 'sympathetic towards hedgehogs'.[9]

There is an exception to this dearth of hedgehog poetry and that comes in the form of the anthology complied as a fundraising book published in 1992 for the British Hedgehog Preservation Society. *Prickly Poems* has some delightful contributions to the form and is also illustrated by a wonderfully diverse crowd of artists. The poems were all written specifically for the book, because none of the authors had any prewritten hedgehog verse, again indicating that there has really not been a great deal of poetical attention paid to the animal.

Hedgehog Dances

Underneath the pale magenta moon,
Hedgehog dances to a slow, sad tune
Played by an armadillo band
Sitting on their haunches
In the soft, white sand.

Hedgehog dances
In a circle on the shore,
Holding up his spiny head,
Dabbing with his paw,
Winding as a question mark,
Mournful as a sigh,
Gazing up into the moon
With brightly eager eyes.

'Moon, I love you!' Hedgehog sings,
'Moon I want you near!'
But moon just goes on shining bright
And doesn't seem to hear.

Hedgehog on the long, white beach
Dances out his love,
Moon is silent silver
In the starry sky above.

The tone set here by the poet Andrew Matthews, with its gentle and slightly melancholy air, runs through much of the collection. While some poems do touch on the obvious humour of the animal, it is hard not to smile at a hedgehog. Orange Prize-winner Helen Dunmore again treats us to a very pastoral scene, albeit a modern one with pylons and headlights.

Hedgehog Hiding in Harvest Hills Above Monmouth

Where you hide
    moon-striped grass ripples like a tiger skin
where you hide
    the dry ditch rustles with crickets

where you hide
    the electricity pylon saws and sighs
    and the combine harvester's headlight
    pierces the hedges

where you hide
    in your ball of silence
    your snorts muffled
    your squeaks and scuffles
    gone dumb
        a foggy moon sails over your head
    the stars are nipped in the bud

where you hide
    you hear the white-faced owl hunting
    you count the teeth of the fox.

Apart from gentle humour and pastoral yearnings, another characteristic that predominates with hedgehog verse is eccentricity. And as an ecologist who has spent many hours in the company of hedgehogs, it is interesting how, despite my best intentions to retain objectivity and eschew anthropomorphism, I find myself of a similar opinion. There are few poets today who master eccentricity as well as A. F. Harrold.

Postcards from the Hedgehog

i
Dear Mum,

Beautiful weather.
I saw a fox last night,
Did as you always said
and rolled into a ball.
After a while it went away.
I was a bit scared all the same.
Wish you were here,

love Simon

ii
Dear Mum,

Lovely weather today.
Just saw a really pretty girl.
Not sure how to approach her.
She makes me really shy
but just all warm inside.
I rolled up into a ball.
Wish you were here,

love Simon

iii

Dear Mum,

It's raining today. I ate a slug.
Wasn't as good as the ones
you used to give us.
Tomorrow I think I'll approach the girl.
Perhaps I'll take her a slug.
She makes me ever so nervous.
I rolled up into a ball.
Wish you were here,

love Simon

iv

Dear Mum,

Sun's out again.
This morning I was very brave
and I went to see her.
I edged up very carefully as you suggested,
but when I spoke to her
I discovered she was actually a pine-cone.
I felt very embarrassed.
Rolled up into a ball.
Wish you were here,

love Simon

What do these poems tell us about our attitudes to the hedgehog? There is a quality of mournful romance to many; a quality that has lasted since the nineteenth century. Clearly, there is affection as well. But, given the absence of the hedgehog from many of the 'great' writers' work, there is a sense that the animal was perhaps considered a little trivial or mundane. This is surprising when one considers what a strange animal the hedgehog is – one that is quite unlike anything else in our landscape.

Recently, a hedgehog has topped the literary charts – which are otherwise distinguished by their almost complete lack of hedgehogs. The French author Muriel Barbery's *The Elegance of the Hedgehog* was published in 2008 and has since sold more than 5 million copies worldwide. While there will have been some hedgehog fans disappointed that there was an absence of the actual animals, the book is beautiful enough to win over even the most belligerent. The metaphorical beast comes in the form of a concierge to upmarket apartments in Paris, Renée Michel. And like Isaiah Berlin's own hedgehog, which we shall meet in more detail in the next chapter, she knows one thing, and it is very big. People like her are not supposed to think deeply. But think she does. She is described as having 'the same simple refinement as the hedgehog: a deceptively indolent little creature, fiercely solitary – and terribly elegant'. And while the ending is shocking, in retrospect it is entirely appropriate.

5 Philosophical Hedgehogs

Rarely has a species spawned a philosophical idea. Rarer still is the species that manages to do it twice. But the remarkable hedgehog has inveigled its way into the minds of philosophers and thinkers through the ages and helped generate two very different, yet powerful, ideas.

ARCHILOCHUS

The earliest record of the first 'hedgehog idea' is from the ancient Greek warrior and poet Archilochus (*c.* 680–*c.* 645 BC).

> The fox knows many things, but the hedgehog knows one big thing.

As an idea on its own, it makes sense. From simple observation, the fox is full of tricks and the hedgehog does just one: to roll tightly into a ball and wait for the bothersome vulpine to vanish. In fact, as we saw earlier, this has become a staple theme of folk tales, with the fox being characterized as cunning and boastful and the hedgehog as slow yet wise.

This idea did not stop with the Greeks. It was collected by Erasmus and published in 1500 in his compilation of proverbs, the *Adagia*. A compulsive compiler of adages, Erasmus is reputed to have amassed over 4,500 by his death. Among them is a form of Archilochus' maxim: *Multa novit vulpes, verum echinus unum magnum*. It has also emerged as an Arabic proverb: 'One knavery of the hedgehog is worth more than many of the fox.' All of them capture the essential opposition of clever foxes and wise hedgehogs. But the aphorism really developed a life of its own when, in 1953, Isaiah Berlin took it for the title of a short book, *The Hedgehog and the Fox: An Essay on Tolstoy's View of History*.

Berlin's aim was to outline the fundamental differences between people who are always collecting ideas and those who have a central philosophy to which all their ideas are linked.

> For there exists a great chasm between those, on one side, who relate everything to a single, central vision, one system, less or more coherent or articulate, in terms of which they understand, think and feel – a single, universal, organising principle in terms of which alone all that they are and say has significance – and, on the other side, those who pursue many ends, often unrelated and even contradictory, connected, if at all, only in some de facto way, for some psychological or physiological cause, related to no moral or aesthetic principle.

The hedgehogs are those that grasp a single big idea and are centripetal, whereas the foxes are centrifugal, with scattered or diffused thought. Clearly this can never be a rigid classification but Berlin does provide a summary of the positioning of various thinkers and writers according to this divide:

> Dante belongs to the first category, Shakespeare to the second; Plato, Lucretius, Pascal, Hegel, Dostoevsky,

Nietzsche, Ibsen, Proust are, in varying degrees hedgehogs; Herodotus, Aristotle, Montaigne, Erasmus, Molière, Goethe, Pushkin, Balzac, Joyce are foxes.[1]

As the purpose of the essay was to fathom the intellectual taxonomy of Tolstoy it is striking to note that he was difficult to classify: Berlin described Tolstoy as by nature a fox who wanted to be a hedgehog. Berlin's idea might have stopped there, but was soon picked up by diverse interests, from headline writers to business gurus. In 1980, for example, Edward L. Walker's book *Psychological Complexity and Preference: A Hedgehog Theory of Behavior* concluded that foxes are the sort of people who have more solutions than they have problems – a fine description of the busy and often contradictory approach of many foxes. The hedgehogs, less exciting perhaps, have the stability of the central vision and organizing principle.

The *Hedgehog Review* was set up in 1999 by the University of Virginia's Institute for Advanced Studies in Culture and has been well read and well respected ever since. It publishes essays and reviews by leading scholars and cultural critics on contemporary cultural change and its wide-ranging individual and social consequences. The central idea is to deliver commentary on the most important questions of our time: what does it mean to be human? How do we live with our deepest differences? When does a community become a good community? Given the wide-ranging nature of these inquiries it would suggest that some foxes are allowed under the cover of the magazine as well.

One of the best-selling hedgehog-motivated publications to have had its origins in Archilochus comes from the successful business consultant Jim Collins. In 2001 he published *Good to Great: Why Some Companies Make the Leap . . . and Others Don't.*

Never let it be said that the hedgehog has not scaled intellectual heights . . . the *Hedgehog Review* asks the deepest questions: what does it mean to be human? How do we live with our deepest differences?

Rock formation in the shape of a hedgehog.

Still selling well more than ten years on, it was the result of five years' work looking at the common factors shared by leading companies. One of the crucial aspects is, unsurprisingly, the quality of a hedgehog. Collins's 'Hedgehog Concept' for success requires the intersection of the answers to three questions: what are you passionate about? What can you be the best at? What can actually make you a living? Collins is calling on people to focus and find the one thing that drives them – their own hedgehog idea.

In turn, Collins has inspired others to follow the hedgehog path. Brian Williamson, for example, runs the 'hedgehoghaven' blog, which is nothing to do with rescuing abandoned beasts.

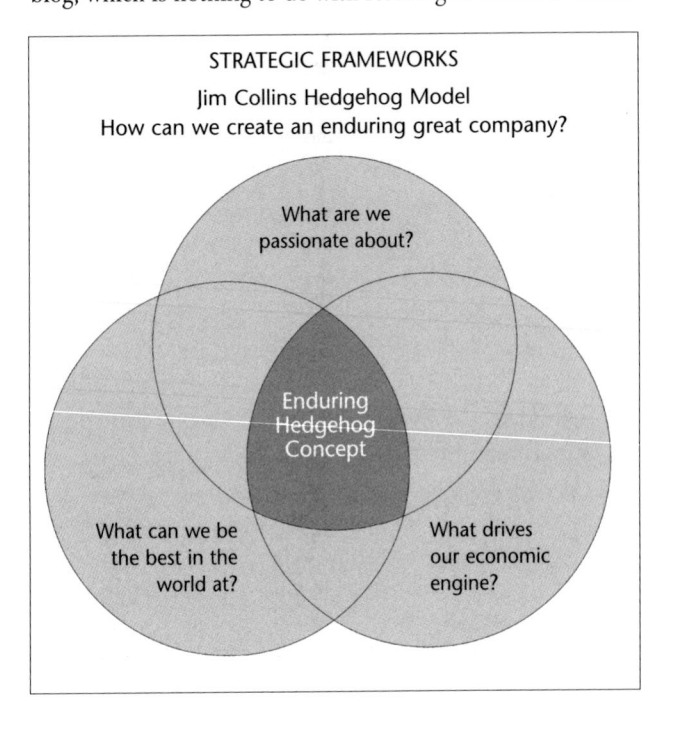

STRATEGIC FRAMEWORKS
Jim Collins Hedgehog Model
How can we create an enduring great company?

What are we passionate about?

Enduring Hedgehog Concept

What can we be the best in the world at?

What drives our economic engine?

Three circles of the hedgehog concept from Jim Collins.

Here he identifies the hedgehogs in theology, leadership, discipleship, Church and culture. Williamson uses the same argument as Collins but moves from business into theology.

Business is not the only sector of society to have made merry with the Archilochus/Berlin formulation. For example, Arianna Huffington speculated in the *Huffington Post* on 'Why America is Deeply in Need of a Good Hedgehog'. For those hedgehogs with ideas above their station there must be some excitement at the declaration that 'the American people are longing for a hedgehog at the helm'. Huffington suggests that President Obama can be a hedgehog – it is how he won office – but that he has since become more vulpine in the style and direction of his political leadership. Unfortunately for the u.s., she concludes that 'our problems are too big to be solved by a fox'.[2]

Archilochus and Berlin also provide the starting point for a short discussion in the journal *Neuroethics and International Biolaw*, titled 'Hedgehogs, Aristotle, and Ritalin', in which a clear distinction between hedgehog and fox thinking is presented.

> A hedgehog is focused on one thing and sees unity, a fox, on the other hand, is focused on many things and engages in distinctions. Put another way, a hedgehog believes that education should be 'an inch wide and a mile deep'. A fox, on the other hand, believes that education should be 'a mile wide and an inch deep.'[3]

The question being tackled is whether Attention Deficit Hyperactivity Disorder (ADHD) needs to be medicated with Ritalin. ADHD is about as un-hedgehog-like a condition as you can get. It is the conclusion of 'Hedgehogs, Aristotle, and Ritalin' that creating a hedgehog through medication leads to a loss of natural ability.

One of the most interesting departures for the hedgehog comes with the eminent legal philosopher Ronald Dworkin's *Justice for Hedgehogs* (2011). While this book clearly upset some of the hedgehog-rights brigade in not being a call to arms for their spiny comrades, it might just have more use for whole of hedgehog-kind should its central ideas become commonly adopted. The one big thing that Dworkin knows is that 'The truth about living well and being good and what is wonderful is not only coherent but mutually supporting: what we think about any one of these things must stand up, eventually, to any argument we find compelling about the rest.' Or, more simply put, 'ethical and moral values depend on one another'.

Dworkin's overall thesis is that 'the fox has ruled the roost in academic and literary philosophy for many decades . . . Hedgehogs seem naive or charlatans, perhaps even dangerous.' This book tackles such a mountain range of ideas: indeed, the chapters range from 'Truth in Morals' to 'Conceptual Interpretation', 'Dignity', 'Obligations' and 'Democracy' and concludes with 'Dignity Indivisible'. This epilogue is the pulling together of the big idea, the hedgehog moment. And at times it feels like there is more of a fox at work, given the range of debate. But the core is returned to each time: the hedgehog knows one very good thing.

> We wanted to vindicate a hedgehog's search for justice in a much more inclusive theory of ethics and morality . . . Someone who lives well when he senses and pursues a good life for himself and does so with dignity: with respect for the importance of other people's lives and for their ethical responsibility as well as his own . . . we must each do what we can to make our own life as good as it could have been. You live badly if you do not try hard enough to make your life good.

Perhaps surprisingly, the hedgehog is riding the crest of a popular wave, and in his closing comments Dworkin brings the philosophical discourse back to earth.

> Cultures have tried to teach a malign and apparently persuasive lie: that the most important metric of a good life is wealth and the luxury and power it brings . . . Nothing better illustrates the tragedy of an unexamined life: there are no winners in this macabre dance of greed and delusion . . . The ridiculous dream of a princely life is kept alive by ethical sleepwalkers. And they in turn keep injustice alive because their self-contempt breeds a politics of contempt for others. Dignity is indivisible.[4]

It seems that the fox–hedgehog axis will continue to provide inexhaustible potential for headline writers and business gurus for many years to come.

RONALD DWORKIN

JUSTICE FOR HEDGEHOGS

Not the book I thought it was, but all the more interesting for that. Pulling together the biggest ideas that face humanity, it is clear that hedgehogs are crucial to a good life.

SCHOPENHAUER

The other significant philosophy to feature a hedgehog emerged from Arthur Schopenhauer. In his collection of philosophical reflections *Parerga und Paralipomena* ('Appendices and Omissions', 1851), Schopenhauer posits that when two hedgehogs huddle together for warmth their spines inflict pain, but when they separate they start to feel cold and so return, get hurt, and retreat until they can find a optimal distance. This is what Schopenhauer calls the 'hedgehog's dilemma'.

His assertion is that this is how humans experience love; as we meet our desire to get as close as possible to the one we love we become more vulnerable to pain. This pushes us away, but then we feel lonely and return to where the pain begins. Our dilemma, like the hedgehog, is how to find our comfort zone. The depressing conclusion of this is the suggestion that human intimacy is always threatened by mutual harm and that the only way to avoid harm is to be cautious and form weak relationships, though the gratification arising from the level of intimacy a strong relationship presents is, in many people's view, worth the potential for pain; this idea has fed a seam of melancholic art, as we shall see later.

Nicholas Wade and his colleagues capture, in the illuminating series *Portraits of European Neuroscientists*, a key essence of the famously pessimistic Schopenhauer:

> The motive force for the individual will is the struggle to survive. Rather than being under the control of the intellect, rational thought is subservient to the will, which is driven by irrational forces. Life is considered to be a succession of blind impulses, like hunger and sexual desire, that are temporarily satisfied, only to return. Pleasure, the satisfaction of an impulse, is transitory: 'No attained object of desire can give lasting satisfaction, but merely a fleeting gratification'.[5]

In some instances the species has been altered while the fundamental nature remains. So, for example, the psychotherapist Deborah Anna Luepnitz's book *Schopenhauer's Porcupines: Intimacy and Its Dilemmas* takes the heart of the 'hedgehog's dilemma' idea into an analysis of five case studies.

A very interesting take on the concept comes from the 'leadership theoretician' Manfred F. R. Kets de Vries's *The Hedgehog Effect*. Published at the end of 2011, this book is a fairly academic tool for coaches and other team leaders. De Vries describes his view with unashamed vigour:

Suggestions that Arthur Schopenhauer chose hedgehogs to explain our greatest dilemma simply because of his hairstyle receive more credibility given this image.

Why do so many teams fail to live up to their promise? Because of the obstinate belief that human beings are rational entities. And because team designers fail to take into account the subtle, unconscious dynamics that influence human behavior.

Coaches, consultants, and executives working with groups and teams are often alerted to the elephants in the room – but what about the hedgehogs? . . . For human

The cast of the Japanese anime *Neon Genesis Evangelion*.

hedgehogs, this conundrum – our simultaneous need for closeness and distance – is a fundamental reason why people often find it so difficult to work successfully in groups and teams.

However, the ability to work well in teams is essential in modern organizations and the price tag of dysfunctional teams can be staggering.

The 'hedgehog's dilemma' has gone on to appear in a number of forms, for example as the title of an episode of *Neon Genesis Evangelion*, a massively popular Japanese anime series. With an apocalyptic plot based around mechanized weapons – giant humanoids, piloted by teenagers, called Evangelions, and their attempt to defeat the hostile attentions of the Angels – it was perhaps an unexpected reference. But the idea runs through the episode with clarity. Its protagonist Shinji Ikari fears that those close to him will be hurt so plans to run away, but reconsiders at the last moment, bringing him back to a place where he may cause and suffer more pain.

Hedgehog philosophy might have seemed an unlikely discipline, but these two colossal and complex ideas have proved that the animal, while not riding high in terms of more conventional appreciation, has managed to make quite an impact intellectually. Both concepts continue to influence thinking in many other spheres of life as well, not least in the arts.

6 Artistic Hedgehogs

The hedgehog suffers in art from its lack of grandeur. There are few magnificent images, majestic operas or mainstream films that feature the animal. The hedgehog in art, as in life, remains mostly hidden in the margins. But, as in the real world, the hedgehog can be found, if you are willing to hunt for it, in some quite extraordinary places.

The dearth of hedgehogs in movies is substantial, unless you allow references to the porn star Ron Jeremy. Appearing in a record breaking 2,000 adult films, Jeremy attained his nickname – 'The Hedgehog' – after coming down with hypothermia on his way to shoot a film called *Olympic Fever* in 1979. Following a long, hot, restorative shower, he emerged pink-skinned but with all his ample body hair erect. The director of the shoot said, 'You are a hedgehog, my friend. A walking, talking hedgehog.'[1]

We have already seen how our view of the hedgehog was altered by the whimsy of Beatrix Potter. But this is not the only vision of hedgehogs to be found in Europe. One of the most extraordinary cinematic representations of the animal comes from Poland, in the feature-length animation *Jeż Jerzy* (*George the Hedgehog*), which received its UK premiere at the London International Animation Festival at the Barbican in 2011. Springing into motion from a long-running cartoon strip of the same name, George is a foul-mouthed hedgehog with voracious appetites –

not for the more traditional macro-invertebrates, but for strong liquor and women. He shows a particular fondness for Yola, a married woman who has a passionate affair with the frequently inebriated hedgehog. He also spends much of the film being chased by two racist skinheads and a mad genetic scientist. It is worth watching, and it does make some sort of warped sense, with the scene following the destruction of a sex shop, which leaves the Warsaw air filled with a fleet of inflatable dolls, a surreal highlight.

Residents of Poland will understand the subtler references to the political situation there and a speaker of Polish will be assaulted by an expletive-laden script that was toned down in the subtitles. The film's director Wojtek Wawszczyk explained in 1994 that the comic strip had originally been aimed at children and was more of a fairy tale, published in the magazine *Świerszczyk*. However, in 1996 this mutated into an adult version, moving to the magazine *Śizg*. 'It's not connected to any cultural circumstances', Wawszczyk explained.

> The title of the comic as well as the film is based on a simple game of words. The word 'Hedgehog' in Polish sounds very similar to a Polish version of the name 'George': 'Hedgehog' is 'Jeż' (pronounced 'Yezh') and 'George' is 'Jerzy' (pronounced 'Yezhee'); here's the whole secret – 'Yezh Yezhee'.

This makes one wonder whether this might explain the magic of Beatle George Harrison. There is some suggestion that Harrison as a name emerged from *hérisson*, the French for hedgehog, making George a potential double hedgehog.

A more genteel filmic imagining of the hedgehog appeared in Russia in 1975, when Yuriy Norshteyn directed *Hedgehog in the*

Ron Jeremy, 'The Hedgehog', has the dubious record of having starred in more adult films than anyone else.

Fog. This ten-minute short film has achieved iconic status and is commemorated in postage stamps and a book of the same name. The little hedgehog has even turned up in graffiti. The story of the animated film is simple but touching. A little hedgehog is on his way to visit his friend the bear cub. Every evening they usually sit together and drink tea from the bear's samovar, heated over a fire of juniper twigs, talk and count the stars. But this time, as the hedgehog heads out with a gift of a jar of raspberry jam, the fog descends. Curious and scared, bedevilled by an ominous eagle owl (a hedgehog predator), he continues and, on seeing a white horse, wonders whether it would drown should it fall asleep in the fog.

The mysterious quality of the animation proved an inspiration for the video to the song 'Human Behaviour' by the Icelandic musician Björk. The hedgehog's adventures continue with dream-like fears in the fog, but all ends well as the two friends meet up and contemplate the goodness of being together. Sergey Kozlov,

The mutated clone of George the Hedgehog has many of the original's bad habits, but is much worse.

115

who originally wrote *Hedgehog in the Fog,* reunited the hedgehog and the bear in at least two other animated short films: *How the Hedgehog and the Bear-cub Changed the Sky,* whose hedgehog is not quite as endearing as that of *Hedgehog in the Fog,* but is another warped and warping tale all the same; and *The Hedgehog and the Christmas Tree* (1975), in which a hedgehog fulfils the yearning of the bear by pretending to be a Christmas tree.

The hedgehog had other Russian advocates too; the author Vladimir Suteev incorporated them into many of his tales, one of which, at least, was made into a film: *The Magic Wand.* In this film the other protagonist is a slightly arrogant rabbit, while the wand in question is the stick that the inspired little hedgehog uses, rather like a pole vaulter, to keep up with the bounding rabbit, and eventually to save it from the jaws of the traditional enemy of the fox.

Both the Israeli and Spanish versions of *Sesame Street* feature, as one of their main characters, a hedgehog. Kipi- Ben-Kipod, a giant hedgehog, has the role of Big Bird in Israel's *Rechov Sumsum,* as well as in *Shalom Sesame,* a Jewish version made and broadcast in the U.S. Espinete is the main character in *Barrio Sésamo,* Spain's version of the show. A large pink hedgehog, Espinete (meaning 'little spine'), used to live in the forest with other hedgehogs, but moved into the Sesame *barrio* and took up residence in the garage of one of the houses.

Aimed at a more adult audience, the experimental short film *Siilijuttu* (*The Hedgehog Thing*) by the Finnish director Esa Illi was released in 2006. In fact, it seems that Finland has a bit of a thing for the hedgehog: in 2004 there was *Jäniksen ja siilin kilpajuoksu* (*The Track-Race of a Rabbit and a Hedgehog*), while before that, in 1983, there was *Minä, siili ja trumpetti* (*The Hedgehog, the Trumpet and Me*). Another unexpected brace of films comes from South Korea. In a Korean release of 1977, *Goseum dochi,* a detective nicknamed 'The Hedgehog' goes to Tokyo and ends up in a kung-fu showdown with a communist spy, 'The Golden Bracelet'. Later in the same year the character appeared in *Jesambudu goseum dochi* (*The Hedgehog of the Third Dock*).

IN MUSIC

There are a few popular references to hedgehogs in song, the most famous probably being from the British psychedelic group The Incredible String Band, whose single 'The Hedgehog Song' is beautiful. It made such an impact on the former archbishop of Canterbury, Rowan Williams, that he chose it as one of his Desert Island Discs on BBC Radio 4 in 2002. A bookish man, Williams was never keen on popular music but was given this single as a 21st-birthday present. The words, in particular of the chorus, proved haunting to him – a very powerful summing up of the problems people have with relationships and life in general.

Mike Heron, the composer of the song, has the unassuming wisdom of many who survived the ravages of the cultural revolution at the end of the 1960s. The choice of the hedgehog was a little accidental. He needed an animal narrator for the song, to chide him for his lack of commitment in a relationship with a beautiful French girl. Retrospectively, Heron admits, the hedgehog has grown on him, becoming utterly perfect for its role in the song. 'There is something about the hedgehog that punches well above its weight', he said.[2] When you consider the impact it has had on the world of philosophy, this is a sentiment that is not so hard to agree with.

Nearly every word of 'The Hedgehog Song' that was referred to in Terry Pratchett's *Wyrd Sisters* cannot be repeated here. Even the title of the song, regularly sung by the drunken witch Nanny Ogg, needs forewarning: 'The Hedgehog Can Never Be Buggered

Rock guitarist and animal rights campaigner Brian May shocked many when he played at the closing ceremony of the London Olympics and revealed politically motivated images of a fox and a badger on his costume. Most people missed the hedgehog on his back. I didn't.

At All'. In fact, the song does not appear at all in the books, but its lyrics have been created by Pratchett fans in a most organic manner, growing with new verses that investigate various species' potential for bestial relationships, concluding with the title of the song in each chorus. Perhaps the strangest recording found on the Internet was from a close-harmony barbershop quartet. Orchestrated by Warren Mars, this song is also available for use in karaoke with a version online to which you can add your own words.

This song has taken on a serious side, too; the impregnable appearance of the hedgehog's posterior has led to the animal becoming the unofficial mascot of the forensic nurses of Colorado in the United States. They argue that, since the majority of victims they deal with have been subject to sexual violence, it is a small relief to find an animal for whom 'no means no'. All a female hedgehog has to do is to frown to draw an end to any unwanted sexual encounter.

The rapper Alex Frecon has produced a wonderful EP called *The Hedgehog Dilemma*. He explained to me where the idea came from:

It is probably the idea of the dilemma more than the hedgehog itself that makes the animal of interest to musicians – at least in the case of dance music. Both Alex Frecon and Maxis produce music that a hedgehog would be hard-pushed to dance to.

What I like about the Hedgehog's Dilemma is that it points out how there is always pain in love . . . But to not accept love, to just isolate yourself out of fear . . . isn't that worse? . . . If I embrace what I love – if I embrace my music, I will undoubtedly be hurt. People will tell me I suck – I will be under constant stress and will most likely never make millions. As a rational person I understand this. But, would it be worse to not embrace my music? Would I freeze to death without it? I think so. I need music in my life – I need it to live.

Another young musician to be troubled by the hedgehog's dilemma is the Macedonian techno artist Jani Galbov, performing as Maxis. He too found himself in a space that was well described by Schopenhauer's idea, saying that 'if someone has enough internal warmth, they can avoid society and the giving and receiving of psychological discomfort that results from social interaction.' And it is with that sentiment that he has applied himself to his music.[3]

Perhaps the biggest musical hedgehog of the moment comes from China, where a certain 'noise-pop' band has been making something of an impact. Formed in 2005, they eschewed the Pinyin version of their name, *ci wei*, to stick with the English 'Hedgehog'. I met them in their home of Beijing in 2007 and was struck by their determination to succeed. All three members still had 'day jobs' and they were working hard to get heard. Since then they have been off on tour around the u.s., thrusting their Ramones- and New Order-influenced music at excitable audiences. On drums and vocals is an unexpectedly delicate young woman called Atom who belies her size with a powerhouse of rhythm. But it was guitarist and singer ZO who explained the origin of the name.

It is a very individual animal. If it doesn't want to interact with the world, it retreats into its protective coat. But he can be friendly if he wants. Sometimes I can be just like that. I can retreat and get rather prickly. But the main reason why I like the hedgehog is that this is a small animal that really knows how to look after itself.

Atom, however, was convinced that there was more to it than that; she reiterated what we have already seen: that there is a profound appreciation of the hedgehog in parts of China. 'We must not ignore the fact that it is a spiritual animal', she said. 'It is an animal to be treated with respect.'

This is not how the hedgehog was treated in 1980 by the team at *Not the Nine O'Clock News* on BBC television in the musical diversion 'I Like Trucking'. Starting with the demise of a hedgehog under the wheel of a truck being marked with a sticker on the side of the cab, recording casualties in the manner of a First World War fighter pilot, it concludes with a highly memorable sandwich of hedgehog. 'Hedgehog Sandwich' became the title of an audio collection of the comedy show's greatest hits and spawned, among other things, the name of a hip-hop collective based in Wakefield, Yorkshire.

The South Korean band Delight also recorded a track called 'The Hedgehog's Dilemma'. And there is an accompanying video, which can be seen online, that beautifully captures the essence of the conundrum Schopenhauer set; being a hedgehog in love leaves the one you love in pain. It is more melodic than the song of the same title by the American heavy metal band Postman Syndrome, but perhaps not as obviously accessible as the music of the Japanese band The Dilemma of Hedgehog, who have been contributing a mix of dance, punk and emo since 2005.

Perhaps surprisingly, a hedgehog has made it into opera and ballet. The ballet representation is of Mrs Tiggy-Winkle again and is from *The Tales of Beatrix Potter*, a film from 1971 that has also been performed as a stage ballet. Separately, though, I have not come across any performances of *The Enchanted Hedgehog: An Opera for All Sizes in Five Scenes* by the twentieth-century composer Cesar Bresgen; whether the lack of favour for the piece is to do with the music or with Bresgen's

dubious fame as one of Adolf Hitler's favourite composers, I do not know.

Librettist Donald Sturrock took inspiration from Roald Dahl's story *Fantastic Mr Fox* and, with the music of Tobias Picker, created a wondrous world. But, despite national admiration on tour with the English Touring Opera, there is a rather serious flaw. See if this excerpt from the closing duet of the show, a duet that drifts into the world of Sophie and Octavian who tumbled into love during Richard Strauss's *Der Rosenkavalier*, reveals it:

MISS HEDGEHOG Is this the one . . .
PORCUPINE . . . that I've waited for?
MISS HEDGEHOG I feel a tingling . . .
PORCUPINE . . . I never felt before.
MISS HEDGEHOG Could it be him?

PORCUPINE Could it be her?

MISS HEDGEHOG I feel excited.

PORCUPINE I feel insecure.

MISS HEDGEHOG He's spiny handsome!

PORCUPINE She's prickly bliss!

MISS HEDGEHOG His eyes are sparkling.

PORCUPINE She's too good to miss.

MISS HEDGEHOG Can it be true?

PORCUPINE Things are moving fast.

MISS HEDGEHOG Is it me and you?

PORCUPINE This is love at last.

TOGETHER Hand in hand, foot in foot, over
leaf, over stone
We will wander together, sleep never alone –
Though our quills may go grey and our
prickles fall out,
We will grow old together, always snout
to snout!

Of course, going back to the opening of this book and the basics of taxonomy, hedgehogs and porcupines are from very different lineages, being of the orders Eulipotyphla and Rodentia respectively. The librettist has been informed.

All of these illustrations of the hedgehog in song are but small beer compared to the most significant artistic hedgehog. And like the real animal, his musical representative did not thrust itself into the limelight. It took a supporting role to one of the greatest composers, Johannes Brahms (1833–1897). While Brahms's music has latterly been considered radical, he was a person of conservative habits. One of these was a daily visit to a tavern in Vienna. It is claimed he would eat nowhere else. And the name of this place? Zum Roten Igel – The Red Hedgehog. It is for this reason that many images of the great composer show him with a small red hedgehog. The most famous is by the Austrian silhouette artist Otto Böhler, who cast him with striking beard, hands characteristically clasped behind his back, and a small hedgehog as companion. The restaurant also sustained other eminent Viennese figures, with Schubert, Schumann and Mendelssohn also regulars. So it is a great shame that the tavern has long since been destroyed. The idea, at least, lives on, however; in Highgate, north London, Clare Fischer decided to take inspiration from Vienna and establish a venue that offers an intimate chamber music experience. And who knows what future greats have already blessed the stage of this Red Hedgehog?

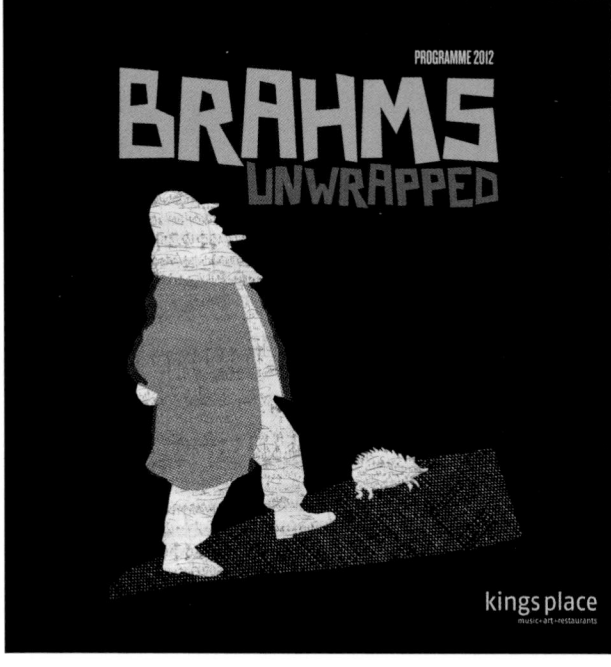

Johannes Brahms's fondness for the restaurant the Red Hedgehog was developed into the narrative for the poster advertising a year of his music at Kings Place in London.

Perhaps as far removed from the elegance of Brahms as it is possible to be, there has been a move to capture the more assertive nature of the hedgehog in a cartoon strip that would have Mrs Tiggy-Winkle running for cover. Milla Paloniemi's *The Cursing Hedgehog* features an animal with an extraordinary amount of anger and a great variety of expletives. Paloniemi is a graphic designer from Helsinki. Her hedgehog emerged while doodling to pass her time, bored in a History of Art class. 'A comic strip where a little angry hedgehog refuses to eat worms! I don't remember where or why it came from but for some reason I wanted to draw it', she explained. 'I put a few of the strips up on the internet without any intention of following up on them, but I kept getting requests to draw more and now, well, they appear in newspapers and I am working on my sixth album.' Her work has won awards and been at the top of the best-seller list in Finland – and all from a foul-mouthed hedgehog!

A more placid cartoon hedgehog comes from New Zealand: Burton Silver's *Bogor* is a lumberjack, living alone out in the forest, whose only friend is a fine hedgehog. There is a great deal of light-hearted philosophizing as the two gaze up at the stars, though they have a very different take on marijuana, crops

While there is a theme of gentleness in most representations of the hedgehog, the cartoonist Milla Paloniemi has identified another side to their nature with her *The Cursing Hedgehog* strip, which runs in papers in her native Finland.

Hedgehogs have relatively small brains.

WHAT THE F*** ARE YOU LOOKING AT ?!?

of which appear to spring up all over the place, resulting in a very contented hedgehog and a slightly irate woodsman. It feels rather like the clash between the establishment and youth of the human world.

Silver's hedgehog is one of many to make its way into the philatelic world. *The Hedgehog in the Fog* is there too, along with stamps from Israel, East Germany, Russia, Hungary, Ukraine, Finland, Guinea, Malta, Zambia, Mali, Sweden, Guernsey, South Africa, the UK and the U.S. While many of the images used bear some relevance to the country in question, some are unexpected. For example, the use of a very European scene, with beech trees, bluebells, fly agaric fungi and butterfly, all set the two European hedgehogs off in a fine manner on the stamp from the Republic of Mali. The wide spread of the hedgehog is yet more proof of the international appeal of this unlikely icon.

In paintings, too, hedgehogs have tended to play the role of supporting actors to the scene. And frequently they reveal how little the artist knew about the animal. Many painted hedgehogs appear disturbingly malformed; for example, Albertus Seba (1665–1736), in his *Thesaurus*, depicted diverse hedgehogs that are clearly drawn from poorly stuffed models.

Stuffing posed a problem to taxidermists which was then passed down to unwitting artists using the stuffed animals to draw from. The skin of a dead hedgehog is deceptive. The skirt of skin that hangs down around a hedgehog, giving it the peculiar impression of being a clockwork toy when it walks, is there to enable it to roll completely into a ball of protective spines. But when unknowing taxidermists are confronted with the skin, the tendency is to fill it, thus creating rather inflated versions of the hedgehog with the legs sticking out at each corner. Other artists who were tricked by this include Carl Oswald Rostosky, who painted *Two Rabbits and a Hedgehog* in 1861. In this not only is the hedgehog rather inflated, but the rabbits look rather unusual too, one certainly seeming to be inspired in part by a wallaby.

A counter to the absence of hedgehogs in high art has come from the brilliant Elvan Alpay, whose recent exhibition in the Galeri Nev in Istanbul is called 'Kirpi', meaning 'Hedgehog'. The exhibition name was a response to her sculptures; 'the paintings came later, inspired by the sculpture', she said. 'All forms of nature are like musical notes from which I compose my work.' The paintings of hedgehogs marry aboriginal abstraction with realistic representation to beautiful effect; there is a lightness to the pictures alongside something very primal. The lightness is interesting, as Alpay was painting through a period of melancholia. 'People say that your work reflects your mental state but

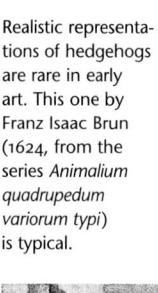

Realistic representations of hedgehogs are rare in early art. This one by Franz Isaac Brun (1624, from the series *Animalium quadrupedum variorum typi*) is typical.

I am not convinced. My work requires an immersion in nature and I do believe that nature is the cure.'

I asked Elvan whether her interest in the hedgehog was inspired by Turkish culture. 'I can only say that, to my surprise, hedgehogs are not animals much appreciated in Islam', she said. 'And that has its effects on Turkish culture.' It seems the inspiration may be more immediate. 'I live very close to the forest and get a chance to encounter them now and then, and I did regularly feed a hedgehog until it decided to leave last summer.'

Elvan's sculptures are on a rather smaller scale than those by the Minimalist sculptor Richard Serra. He has titled one of his trademark controversial assemblages of sheet metal *The Hedgehog and the Fox*. The three vast ribbons of steel were erected in 2000 in the campus of Princeton University. Standing 5 m high

Hans Hoffman, *A Hedgehog*, before 1584, watercolour.

Hedgehog and insect, from a Turkish illuminated manuscript, 1710s.

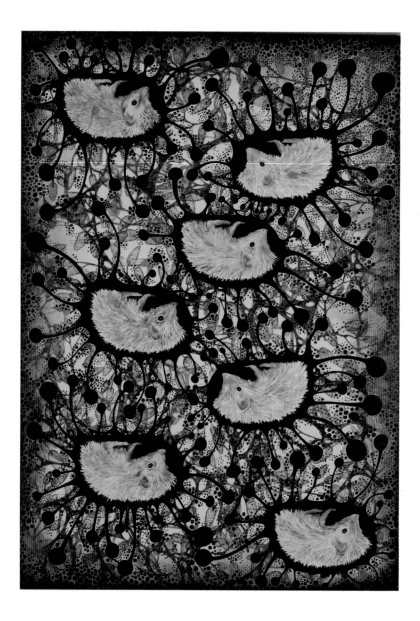

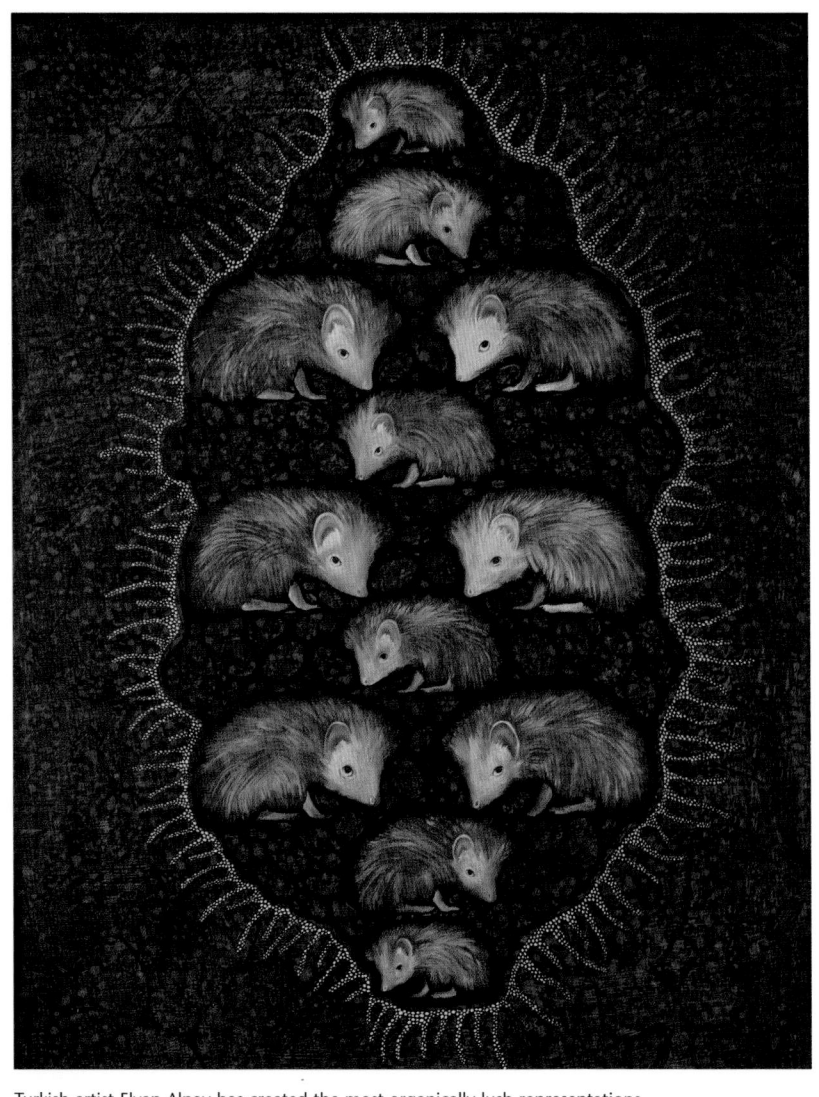

Turkish artist Elvan Alpay has created the most organically lush representations of hedgehogs in a series of images that were exhibited in 2012.

and 30 m long, they are best understood not merely by viewing, but by walking between them, the design allowing you to encounter different glimpses of sky.

Serra's explanation of his work's relationship to Isaiah Berlin's use of the famous quote by Archilochus ties it in with the significance of siting it at a university. 'It points to how scholars either become free thinkers and invent or become subjugated to the dictates of history. This is the classical problem posed to every student.' The sculpture, as with many of Serra's works, was not 'finished'; there was no grinding, polishing or paint used and it was allowed to accumulate the scrapes and scratches of its creation and also to rust in the elements. So much is this the case that the piece swiftly acquired the nickname 'Old Rusty'.

Despite the obvious love people have for the hedgehog, it is interesting that it has rarely appeared in any artform approaching the mainstream. Perhaps the Serra sculpture and Alpay's paintings are as close as it has come. This is because, as mentioned earlier, the hedgehog still remains a 'folk' animal, one that is almost so prosaic as to not warrant the attention of artists. But this has not stopped it being picked up by the world of advertising, perhaps even for the same reasons that sees high art eschew the remarkable animal.

7 Commercial Hedgehogs

The earliest 'hedgehog' found in the world of commerce and industry seems to be the address of a London publishing company, Willyam (or occasionally Wyllyam) Seres. 'Dwellyng at the West ende of Poules, at the sygne of the Hedgehog' in the sixteenth century, they produced books such as *The Primer Set Furth at Large, with Many Godly and Devoute Prayers* (1559) and *The Burnynge of Paules Church in London in the Yeare of Oure Lord 1561*.

How do companies assign characteristics to animals for their own marketing ends? Do they act with any consistency? At the heart of the advertiser's dream is the plan 'to transfer desirable cultural meanings to products with which they are associated'.[1] So what are the cultural meanings that have been attached to hedgehogs? The hedgehog is commonly used in advertisements and the meanings it is used to represent are widely divergent.

There is evidence that adverts that feature animals score highly in their ability to switch the brand preference of consumers away from competitors.[2] Why is this? It is possibly because we have already attributed certain characteristics to certain animals, so that their appearance in an advert can be a kind of shorthand: we know that bees are industrious, foxes are cunning, doves are peaceful and rats are dirty. But what do we know about the hedgehog?

Being covered in spikes has meant that 'hedgehog' has become shorthand for any prickly product, for example, pipe reamers.

The difficulty in this comes from the inherent paradox; like all animals, there are at least two versions of the beast in our psyche. Bears are soft, bears are dangerous; bees are hard-working, bees will sting. And hedgehogs? Well, they are adorable, cute and cuddly while at the same time being impenetrable balls of spines. Many of the adverts in which they appear play more on hedgehog behaviour than character. And what is the thing that most people associate with hedgehogs? Being run over. So it is rather ironic that hedgehogs have been used to advertise cars.

CARS AND ROADS: IRONIC ADVERTISING

The tyre manufacturer Goodyear took perhaps the most acceptable approach in their television advert of 2009. Three perspectives are combined: the car, moving fast on a wet road;

the scientists monitoring performance on computer screens; and the hedgehog, gently bumbling along. Fortunately the tyres provide '20 per cent shorter braking distance in the wet than competitors after 30,000 km': thus the car stops a few centimetres short of killing the creature. Though the advert was screened across Europe, it is rather frustrating that the species of hedgehog used was not native. It was a domesticated African pygmy hedgehog, probably a cross between at least two *Atelerix* species. (This is a recurrent irritant to the hedgehog pedant. Pet hedgehogs are far easier to train and therefore are better fodder for photographers and film-makers. As the world of marketing is fairly void of hedgehog pedants, this sort of thing slips through frequently.)

In 2011 another tyre manufacturer, Continental, launched a TV and cinema campaign using a very similar story, at least in the detail that matters; this time we see a woman driving her car filled with her sleeping family to within a hair's breadth of squashing a hedgehog. Again, it is not a European hedgehog, despite the market in which the advert was shown. Joy Ann Freytäger, part of the team behind the advert, explained to me that hedgehogs are very difficult to train; the one they used was

The association between risk of death and car tyres is obvious and one that Continental is not alone in exploiting.

the only one available. Apparently this particular hedgehog is not unfamiliar to the advertising world, appearing in other commercials, though they did use a stunt pine cone to assist in framing the shot.

These adverts play on the susceptibility of hedgehogs to becoming two-dimensional and, along with the use of the hedgehog to promote road safety, seem to carry a certain amount of logic. But there are other examples of the use of a hedgehog that seem a little odder. Gas-mask-wearing hedgehogs breathe more easily when a Mercedes goes by in an advert created in 1994 by the Jim Henson Creature Shop. Elsewhere, an early outing for Wallace and Gromit artists Aardman Animations was a 1987 advert promoting a car servicing company, SMC, with a rather flat hedgehog. The car maker Nissan and the Association of French Motorways have also engaged the services of this unlikely hero.

In all of these adverts the real tragedy for hedgehogs is that they are being incorporated into the promotion of an activity directly linked to their demise across Britain, and possibly the rest of Europe. It is not just the death toll on the roads that is the problem, it is the fact that busy roads act as barriers in the wider landscape, fragmenting the habitat of the hedgehog and increasing the risk of a piecemeal extinction, something we will return to later.

There is another conjunction of hedgehog and road that was applied with more benign aims. For many years the Department for Transport in the UK used a family of hedgehogs to teach children about crossing the road. While the series of adverts was well crafted and well received, it struck many that the hedgehog was a poor role model to offer children, as many children will only ever see a real-life hedgehog dead on the roads they are supposed to be teaching them to cross, though the reason the

Department decided to withdraw the campaign in 2008 was that it was aimed at too young an audience. This decision was quickly followed by an online campaign to have the hedgehog reinstated – though this was, unfortunately, unsuccessful.

Perhaps the strangest use of the hedgehog though was in a South African advert for the Ford Focus. A young woman sees a hedgehog lying on the road. She stops her car, goes to the animal and says, 'We need to find a vet.' Looking up she sees that the nearest town is Bietjiekleinfontein, 68 km away. Sat on the lap of her passenger, the hedgehog so enjoys the journey that, following a return trip to its pickup point (it is a good idea to release hedgehogs where you found them, if you can, though releasing them back beside the road is a less brilliant plan), and a slightly sad farewell wave from its 'saviour', the now recovered hedgehog gets up and looks down the road until the correct car comes into view: another Ford Focus. It waddles into the road, swoons and awaits another trip in the comfort of the car. One of

The use of hedgehogs as a road safety icon lasted for many years in the UK, despite the very mixed message it must have given.

the two rescuers says, 'Dad, we need to find a vet', at which point our hedgehog gives a knowing wink to the camera.

The association, however, is clear. Hedgehogs advertise cars because hedgehogs are associated with roads. But that does not stop it seeming slightly odd, in much the same way that turkeys being used to advertise Christmas does. Perhaps more a more obvious association should be the hedgehog's characteristic spines, from which another raft of advertising takes its inspiration.

FROM SPONGES TO BANKS: ADVERTISING

The hedgehog's repertoire is not restricted to motor cars. Easily the strangest campaign has been the long-running series of adverts featuring Ernie the Hedgehog and his fondness for the scourers made by Spontex. Depending on which country the adverts are aimed at, they range from romance to something close to pornography between the hedgehog and the scourer. The campaign originated in France, the home of Spontex, but has spread. Clearly, different cultures are more comfortable with different degrees of intimacy. In the UK the campaign has focused more on the safety of Ernie; in 2009 security guards were hired in a partnership between Spontex and the British Hedgehog Preservation Society to protect a large bonfire at the Three Counties Showground in Malvern, Worcestershire, in the run up to Bonfire Night. Patrolling the grounds with torches, they were there to highlight the tragic problem of bonfires: a brilliant structure for hedgehogs, they tend to appear just around the time of year when the creatures are preparing to hibernate. The consequences are obvious.

Back on safer ground, the hedgehog has found its way into many other products. Some simply use the hedgehog for a play on words – the 'Hedge-Hog' hedge trimmer being an obvious

'Don't Burn Ernie': Spontex-sponsored security guards at the Three Counties Showground, Malvern, prior to Bonfire Night celebrations.

case in point, though the use of hedgehogs in an advert for a Monsanto garden chemical product would have drawn criticism from the hedgehog union, if there was one. It is also possible to implicate the BEWODECK IGEL (*igel* being German for hedgehog) deck-fastening system in the eradication of important hedgehog habitat, as it facilitates the expansion of decking across gardens.

While there might be some logic for marrying hedgehogs with garden products, the tie-in with banking is a little more obscure. For a brief moment it seemed that the hedgehog was going to take over the banking world. First Abbey National in the UK launched a campaign with wonderful television adverts that attracted a great deal of good attention. It opens with two hedgehogs in a woodland; a voiceover says: 'It is frustrating when your ideal home is just out of reach . . .' as a European hedgehog reaches up and tries to get into a hole in a tree stump. But it is too high, so the hog tumbles back down in a ball, rolling some distance before returning with a red cube, itself an icon of the Abbey campaigns. When this has been pushed in place with its snout, the clever hedgehog is able to clamber up into this highly unlikely new home, followed by what one infers is its mate.

So, apart from the nest-site and the use of the box being improbable, and the fact that these are solitary creatures that meet for courtship and then part, this was a step or two above most hedgehog adverts. What was interesting was that these were European hedgehogs that had clearly been trained. Apparently this took some time. But the animals were old hands, having recently starred in *Miss Potter* (2006), a film that, while painting a far more three-dimensional image of Beatrix Potter than a casual reading of her children's books would provide, manages to miss the crucial motivation for her retreat from London: her treatment at the hands of the scientific establishment.

The Abbey National campaign was supplemented by print advertising, in newspapers and magazines as well as posters in the bank branches. It remains a shame that I was not allowed to take ownership of the 5-foot-high hedgehog that greeted me on entering the Oxford branch, though they did allow me a couple of smaller models to keep me quiet.

At around the same time another bank, Icesave, also launched a campaign featuring a hedgehog. Head of marketing at the bank Alan Gilmour said that they had tried to

> develop an advertising style with personality to help . . . us stand out in a cluttered and hugely commoditised market place. We . . . try to find images which reflect our desired personality and which also express something about the message we [are] trying to communicate. We liked the image of the hedgehog because it communicated so well that, with our interest rate guarantee, not only were you well protected as with a hedgehog and its quills but you could afford to put your . . . savings money into hibernation knowing that you would still be protected from cuts in interest rates and that your money would still be getting a great return. The imagery also allowed us to do this in a non clichéd and unbank-like way. In this instance the hedgehog is meant to represent the customer and not the bank.

So the hedgehog as customer motif continues, though unfortunately this time with poor success, as that campaign, from designer Michael Peters, was one of the last run by Icesave before its collapse helped tip the world into an economic whirlpool in October 2008.

The use of a hedgehog in an advert to sell interest in the German company MyStocks is one of the most inventive. An

The now subsumed Abbey National building society no longer offers this deal.

adviser is being asked to suggest a good investment. To identify the best he brings out a hedgehog and a seesaw, and lets loose a handful of balloons. Placing the hedgehog on one side of the seesaw, he propels it upwards with a sharp blow to the other end, whereupon its prickles pop a balloon, releasing a note inside, which identifies the very best option for investment. I think it is possible that chicken entrails might be as effective.

As in the literature and poetry associated with the hedgehog, the same sort of sense of the animal emerges; for many, it seems, the hedgehog sits somewhere between comic and melancholic. There is a put-upon air to many of them that is reminiscent of Stan Laurel at his best; maybe there is something in his famously upstanding haircut?

SONIC, AND OTHER ICONS

Perhaps the most well-known commercial hedgehog, however, suffers from a different problem – mainly that he looks very little like a hedgehog, and more like a blue rat. But Sonic the Hedgehog, 'born' in 1991, is probably the best-known hedgehog in the world. In fact, there are probably more people who have seen Sonic than have seen a real hedgehog. While that is an amazing achievement for Sega, it is also not a little sad. The inevitable question has to be, why a hedgehog? The explanation given to me by the developers still fails to really explain the need:

> The development team (later known as the Sonic Team) was seeking an original action game different from any existing title of other developers. To differentiate the game from others, they set 'speed' as its basic concept and 'exhilaration' from hi-speed dash for its main theme. At first, they came up with a rabbit character, but when they were thinking of an attack method that could support the speedy rhythm of the game, the conclusion they came up with was to 'charge' right into the enemies. Then, they thought again about an animal that can beat enemies by charging into them, and came up with the

From the author's own collection, evidence that toy hedgehogs come in many a shape and form.

idea that a hedgehog covered with spikes can attack enemies by charging right into them and yet keep proceeding in hi-speed. They first had the theme of 'speed', which connected to the action concept of 'charging', and concluded with a hedgehog from that function.

There is a considerable narrative behind the jumping and charging of Sonic. The exhilaration tells a story. For example, in the introduction of the game *Sonic Colours* (2010), we are told:

> The diabolical Dr Eggman has hatched another plan for world domination! He has built an amazing interstellar amusement park, floating in space bursting with incredible rides and attractions. However, all is not as it seems as Dr Eggman has abducted an entire alien race called Wisps from far away planets and is harnessing their Wisp energy and colour power for an evil plan. Before he has time to set his plans in motion . . . Sonic discovers his mysterious theme park and finds he is able to use these new alien powers too! Fuelled by their colourful energy; Sonic embarks on an adrenaline-pumping, super speed adventure through vibrant worlds from candy mountains, to lush vegetation in a mission to halt the sinister plot.

From playing the game, though, it is tricky to tease out the subtleties of the story. Prior to the UK launch, Sega's publicity machine got in touch with the British Hedgehog Preservation Society, along with other carers around the country, asking what they could do to help hedgehogs (and themselves, of course) as a publicity stunt. Plenty of suggestions were put forward – even one to build a hedgehog bridge across the M25 motorway. But

Sonic the Hedgehog.

in the end they went ahead and enraged many with a campaign featuring, once again, an African pygmy hedgehog.

Sonic has been remarkably successful, with over 84 million games sold worldwide in the twenty years to 2011. He has also become the most merchandized of hedgehogs, making his way into toys and on to clothing. He is not alone, though, as a prickly emblem.

Along with teddy bears, hedgehogs seem a favourite of children's clothing designers. Their use ranges from the relatively cartoon-like designs printed on clothes by Next, Mini Boden and Marks

& Spencer, among others, to the delightful pen-and-ink illustration from Belle & Dean's line of organic clothes for children. My only complaint there is that it is not available in adult sizes!

Elsewhere an innovative American company named Shirt Woot! have a system whereby designs are available for a week, but if they have not met the mark from a community of voters, they get dropped permanently. So I was lucky to find a T-shirt featuring a mountainous hedgehog eating a team of construction workers, while it experienced its moment of fame.

Lesser hedgehogs continue to pop up all over the place. The seductive voice that calls a hedgehog over to a plastic bottle of shampoo says, 'Let your stressed hair relax in the forest', while the hedgehog uses the bottle as a shower curtain, emerging with soft, free and airy spines, does so in the name of Mori No Essence from Japan. And while there is a bit of a misunderstanding there as to the purpose of the spines (in that they need to be unrelaxed to be effective), it is nothing to the utter failure to understand the concept of a nocturnal animal. In an NHS antibiotic awareness advert for television, a snuffling cartoon hedgehog comes home and, deciding to follow official advice, does not go looking for antibiotics for its cold, instead taking plenty of fluid and rest, eventually waking in bed as the sun rises. Of course, that is when hedgehogs ought to be going to sleep, giving us a sound scientific sentiment being backed up with complete nonsense.

And while on the subject of nonsense, there seems to be not a little of that behind the branding of a pair of tough trainers designed for running up and down mountains. The Hedgehog, from The North Face, are just that. Like most of these impressions of a hedgehog, the product is about as far removed from the animal itself as possible. Leaping, charging . . . not activities usually associated with the snuffling suburbanite.

MEN'S
HEDGEHOG
II GTX

20%
OFF

WAS £84.99
£67.99

Hedgehog shoes from The North Face are designed for running up and down hills, almost exactly in the way that hedgehogs do not.

ALCOHOLIC HEDGEHOGS

Burton Silver's hedgehog had a preference for marijuana (see chapter Six), but there have also been quite a few adoptions of the animal in support of the alcohol industry. In 2008, the Côtes du Rhone wine industry dropped its highly successful ten-year ad campaign, featuring a hedgehog and a hippo, after concerns were raised that it might be targeting the young. That is not the only vinous connection: the Alpha Estate on the Amyndeon Plateau in northern Greece has produced a wine from the Xinomavro grape that is produced on their 'Hedgehog Vineyard'. In 2010 the estate won a Silver award from *Decanter* magazine, which gave tasting notes of 'elegant strawberries with a touch of new oak, blackcurrants, morello cherry – all very well balanced and satisfying'.

Every now and then a hedgehog beer will appear. One has recently been brewed to celebrate the 30th anniversary of the

British Hedgehog Preservation Society. Brewed by Hobsons, in Worcestershire, it is a deliciously light, bottle-fermented ale. And to sell this beer there should be, and are, hedgehog pubs: The Hedgehog, Lichfield; The Hedgehog Inn, Copthorne, West Sussex; The Dog and Hedgehog in Dadlington, Warwickshire; and The Hedgehog and Pheasant in Pimlico, London, to name but four. And while the reviews of The Hedgehog and Bucket in Belfast were damning, The Hedgehog of Welwyn Garden City, Hertfordshire, seems a cut above the rest, including a pub football team complete with hedgehog mascot.

It is unsurprising that Hertfordshire should host such a hostelry, as the traditional nickname for the people of the county is 'Hertfordshire Hedgehogs'. While it is nice to think that the spiny animals may have had a special place in the hearts of the good people of Hertfordshire, it seems that it is more likely a corruption of the word 'haycock', which means haystack, a reference to the agricultural exports from the county to the growing medieval city of London.

A stronger drink than wine and beer has also attracted the hedgehog branding. A whisky called Hedgehog is, unsurprisingly, made in the French town of Hérisson. (France has a town called 'hedgehog', as does Germany – Igel – yet Britain, with its apparent love of hedgehogs, has no place named after the wonderful animal.) Hérisson's whisky is made of organic ingredients, but is also a little unusual; its maker, Monsieur Balthazar, has gone down the American route of using mostly corn, making Hedgehog whisky more of a bourbon. This decision may have been inspired by the town being home to one of the Bourbonnais castles, built in the fourteenth century. Sadly I did not, having bought a bottle, find the drink very nice.

The Hedgehog, Welwyn Garden City, is one of a few pubs to choose the name.

As a fundraising venture for the British Hedgehog Preservation Society, the production and consumption of beer seems like a win–win situation.

From alcohol to sex and the world of the erotic hedgehog. Unfortunately now, with its stock in decline, one of the most outlandish hedgehog-related companies was the brainwave of blacksmith Brian Sims. Initially he started with the Happy Hedgehog Wrought Iron Works – the name being the choice of his children, for whom he had been making up 'Happy Hedgehog' stories for years. But after a customer's request for more 'interesting' artefacts he set up an additional enterprise, 'Erotic Hedgehog', specializing in 'the bespoke design of wrought iron'. The company makes traditional items such as chandeliers and mirror frames, but also beds, chairs and cages that can be made to order, with points for the attachment of restraints; there are also ball and chains and manacles to choose from.

Brian Sims's company comes from a good line of hedgehog-related forges. People now collect the billhooks and axes that sprang from Cornelius Whitehouse's ironworks in Cannock Chase, Staffordshire, from the middle of the nineteenth century. The connection? Many of the blades are stamped with a little hedgehog. One theory about the origin of this branding was that it acted as a reminder to those wielding slashing instruments to be aware that hedgehogs might be lurking in the brush being cleared.

Back when Whitehouse's blades were first being used, it is probable that any hedgehogs unfortunate enough to get caught a blow would end up in the pot. But there is no evidence of the commercial production of hedgehogs for food, thank goodness. However, this has not kept them away from food altogether. There are the French Petit Hérrison, delightful chocolate and marshmallow biscuits; Old Timers, a Dutch liquorice brand; and, most famously, crisps. Indeed, Hedgehog crisps became quite a news item in the 1980s.

The story began in a pub in Wales in 1981, when a pub landlord named Philip Lewis decided that the world was missing out on 'hedgehog flavoured' crisps and set up Hedgehog Foods Ltd. While he enjoyed the joke, he also ran into problems, ending up in trouble with the guardians of trading standards. In court, evidence was called from a Roma witness, who agreed that the pork flavouring actually used in the crisps was indeed reminiscent of the taste of hedgehog. The case was settled and, as the crisps contained no real hedgehog, they were relabelled as 'hedgehog flavour' crisps.

The behaviour, appearance and perceived character of hedgehogs have all meant that the animal has become one of the most frequently used in advertising. And while there is an obvious contradiction, with this prickly bundle of spines being considered so cute and cuddly, it is perhaps more obvious that the hedgehog

The Hedgehog Forge, established by Cornelius Whitehouse, has stamped a wide range of agricultural tools with this image. This is from my billhook.

There is little not to love with these liquorice sweets from the Netherlands.

Crunchy on the outside and with a magical mix of caramel and marshmallow within, these treats deserve a wider audience.

should rise above so many other animals. Most animals carry contradictory cultural values, but as we have seen, since Beatrix Potter and her makeover of the animal in 1905, the hedgehog has been seen as almost universally good.

8 Domestic Hedgehogs

Hedgehogs are not what one would consider a predictable animal to be domesticated. Humans began domesticating wildlife with the dog, around 9000 BC. It is fascinating that most of the domesticated animals and plants that we use to this day were selected for us during the Neolithic period; Stone Age man gifted the computer generation the building blocks of the wealth our society is built on – originally, livestock and acriculture.

The criteria necessary for an animal to be domesticated, explains Jared Diamond in *Guns, Germs, and Steel* (1997), are:

1. The diet needs to be flexible
2. Growth rate needs to be reasonably fast
3. They need to breed in captivity
4. They need to be not aggressive
5. Their temperament should reduce panic
6. A modifiable social hierarchy

I suppose one should add that the animal ought to present humans with some utility, whether that is as food, fibre or companion.

It is possible to imagine the hedgehog meeting most of the criteria. But why would anyone want to domesticate a hedgehog? There have been attempts to corral the Western European hedgehog to our own ends. But whether should be seen as the early stages of domestication or, as is more likely, as a symbiotic relationship, is hard to tell at this distance.

The Reverend J. G. Wood tried to understand more of these relationships in his book *Petland Revisited* (1903).[1] 'I have endeavoured to demonstrate', he explains in his preface,

> the mental and sympathetic connection which, though so little appreciated, exists universally between man and beast, and is, in fact, the link that unites, through mankind, the spiritual to the material world. Sympathy unites all.

Wood describes himself as having a 'Bohemian love of eccentricity' and a desire to find 'authentic histories of pets which do not belong to the ordinary "domestic animals"'. So it is hardly surprising that he came to the hedgehog, an animal that 'very few persons seem to have taken any interest in'. He appears unsympathetic to the creature, which, he claims, 'does not appear to possess much intellect, and its armoury of sharply pointed prickles renders it unpleasant to handle'. But direct experience improves his disposition towards the animal. On seeing one being carried around by children, and it being on good terms with the house dog, he noticed that when with people it knew, it kept its spines lowered, 'and was as harmless as a rabbit'.

Indeed, Wood reported a letter he received from a woman that casts a different view of the hedgehog; in 1881 she bought one to put in her kitchen cupboard to catch cockroaches. This certainly addresses the issue of utility. After this experiment, Wood's correspondent proceeded to undertake a series of further experiments to see what it is hedgehogs like best to eat. Her hedgehog did not like eggs or apples but happily ate dead mice. And, revealing an interesting, eccentric family, she added,

> My mother had a large pet toad which she had kept for about two years. A few nights after I bought my hedgehog, a sound was heard as of some one eating in a vulgar manner. My mother went to find out what the noise could mean, and in the dim twilight saw the hedgehog with the hind-legs of the toad hanging out of its mouth.

The woman's experiments seemed to conclude that the food her pet found most agreeable was cockroaches – she asserted that her hedgehog can eat about 200 in a meal – which ties in neatly with a note in *The Times* from 11 November 1908, which read: 'Their liking for insects is well known, and they are frequently kept in houses for the purpose of clearing off cockroaches.'

Not everyone was so grounded in their approach to feeding hedgehogs; Reverend Wood reports another woman who had been 'handed' a hedgehog, which she tamed with cooked meat:

> One day his sensitive nostrils detected an unknown scent. He quested about until he discovered a tumbler filled with hot negus. Some of it was offered to him in a spoon, and he took to it so kindly that before long he could not walk, and I had to carry him to bed. Next day, when some negus was offered to him, he refused it indignantly.

Going back to a more conventional diet, *The Times* carried a letter on 17 January 1933 that also indicates the usefulness of the hedgehog.

I do not remember how we came by him, but I do know that we acquired him to make war on the beetles which infested the basement of the house we then lived in London. This he did with complete success, and there was soon not a beetle left. 'Peter' soon became quite tame and would come when he was called with great eagerness when a saucer of milk was offered to him. He also became good friends with our fox terrier, but if a strange dog came to the house his prickles went up at once.

Peter came to a very sad end. It did not occur to us . . . to shut him up in a basket at night. Seeking warmth, he crept into the back of the flues of the kitchen range. There, alas, poor Peter was battered to death when the flues were cleaned in the morning.

While it is true that an irate hedgehog can be moved to biting, this signage might be over-egging that a little.

This letter was just one in a series received by *The Times* in 1933 following a piece in the paper, 'Stachelengro, A Hedgehog in the Family', which revealed the potential for even the European hedgehog to tolerate a little domesticity. Following its rescue by the correspondent from a barrage of barking dogs, the hedgehog was fed, unhealthily as we now know, on bread and milk.

It over-ate itself and was carried dormant upstairs to the drawing room, for fear that the animals, in the absence of their masters, might violate the Pax Britannica which rules over dogs, cats, rabbits, guinea-pigs, tortoises, lizards, and snakes and harm the newcomer ... A short time afterwards a visitor would have been astonished to see a hedgehog calmly lying full length in front of the fire, as if he had been a cat long established in the home.

When the children are at home he is carried up to the nursery and put to bed in a doll's cot, covered with blanket and equipped with pillow ... But he does not only sleep. He grows cheekier and cheekier every day. We had herrings and put a plate of leavings on the floor ... His method of getting his fair share – and a bit more – was quite simple. He marched into the middle of the plate and covered as much food as he could with his hair-fringed, spiny body, while four bewildered cats stood round puzzled. I have seldom seen a better argument against disarmament.

It is fascinating to see a hedgehog featuring in an argument of geopolitical significance. And that was not the only time during the build-up to the Second World War that the papers were graced by a metaphoric hedgehog. On 27 December 1934

The Times carried a report of a speech given by Rudolf Hess in which he introduced a fable from Wilhelm Busch.

> A fox, meeting a hedgehog, said, 'Don't you know that peace has been proclaimed and that it is a crime against the king's command to go armed? Hand over your skin!' Whereupon the hedgehog – answering: 'First have your teeth drawn, then we can talk' – coiled himself into a ball, projected his spikes and 'defiantly faced the world, armed but peaceful!'

So it seems that both sides of the impending disaster considered themselves hedgehogs. If only that had been the case; hedgehogs are brilliant at mutual avoidance.

HEDGEHOGS AS FAD PETS

Notwithstanding these early, and largely accidental, occasions of cohabitation, there has been a serious effort made to domesticate the hedgehog. The exotic pet industry has an aim to generate great excitement and stimulate the popularity of a must-have fad pet. It works periodically; Vietnamese pot-bellied pigs and terrapins, for example. And like all fad pets, just as the interest waxes it also wanes.

So it was that in 1991 a dealer in exotic pets was in Nigeria wondering where the next fad pet might come from when he found a crate full of hedgehogs: exactly which species is not clear, but probably *Atelerix albiventris*, the African pygmy, and *A. algirus*, the Algerian hedgehog. The story the dealer brought back was that the hedgehogs were offered to him by people claiming that the area was overrun with starving hedgehogs and they were doing the hedgehogs a favour by finding them a new

home. Some people find this idea a little unlikely. But the pet Hedgehog charmer in India. dealer, Richard Stubbs, did think that with their undeniably cute looks, they might just work, so he bought 2,000 of them at 50 cents each and shipped them to New York, where they sold fast.[2] By his account he shipped around 50,000 hedgehogs to the United States, and other dealers another 30,000, before the authorities noticed that the animals carry foot-and-mouth disease and ended the trade as a preventative measure in 1994.

By this point hedgehogs had become the fad pet of the moment. Prices rose and with that people's desire to capitalize on the investment they had made in their new pet: owners became breeders, and prices continued to rise. An organization set up to help people with their hedgehogs, trumpeted: 'Your best returns are with the North American Hedgehog Association.'

Some newspapers were explicit. 'Move Over, Pot-bellied Pigs: Here Come the Hedgehogs', ran the *Seattle Times* in 1995. Motivation was straightforward; *Pet Product News* headed an article titled 'u.s. Pet Retailers Watch Exotic Hedgehog Prices Soar'. 'Tiny Pets are Big Business', ran another paper. But it was the *Washington Post* that revealed, unwittingly, the start of a considerable problem, with one dealer reported as 'selling [hedgehogs] for $188. Just a few months ago . . . they were selling for up to $500, but now more breeders are getting into the act and the supply has increased.'

The problem is that when wildlife gets turned into a commodity to be traded, greed takes over. The organization TRAFFIC, which monitors the world trade in wildlife, recorded a breeding pair of these animals selling for around $4,500 in 1995, and the most expensive they found was a pair for $5,500. The inflated prices were caused by the expectation that these new must-have pets would continue to sell and therefore generate a return on the massive investment. So at these prices the animals had to work hard at reproduction to ensure a profit, which meant a certain disregard for hedgehog husbandry set in, with devastating consequences.

Since there was a restricted breeding pool, it was not unexpected when a lethal, congenital condition started to emerge, named 'wobbly hedgehog syndrome' (WHS, an unfortunate name, probably given by someone with an overdeveloped sense of literalness who was unaware that giving a humorous name to a deadly disease would not necessarily increase sympathy). The condition causes the hedgehogs to gradually lose motor function, generating the wobbling, leading to incapacitation and death within six months. No hedgehogs have survived WHS. Although it has not been found in wild populations of hedgehogs, there were some breeders who rejected the idea that the massive amount of inbreeding was the cause of the problem. Nonetheless there is now a widespread effort to remove carriers of the disease from the breeding pool.

Africa was not the only potential source of hedgehogs. A request from an exotic pet breeder in Canada to a hedgehog carer in Lincolnshire for a supply of European animals was firmly rebuffed. Whatever one's views about the rights and wrongs of taking a wild animal as a pet, there are really good reasons why the European hedgehog would make a particularly poor choice, not least of which is their more fluid faeces.

The craze, like all crazes, peaked and fell. But a hard core of devotees remained and still remains, keeping faith in the wonders of pet hedgehogs. Periodically they gather and around 100 hedgehog shows have taken place since the first in Tacoma, Washington, in October 1995. Every other October one of the biggest takes place in Denver, Colorado, and attracts people and their hedgehogs from all over North America. The weekend event has two key components: the International Hedgehog Association's Conformation Show and the International Hedgehog Olympic Games.

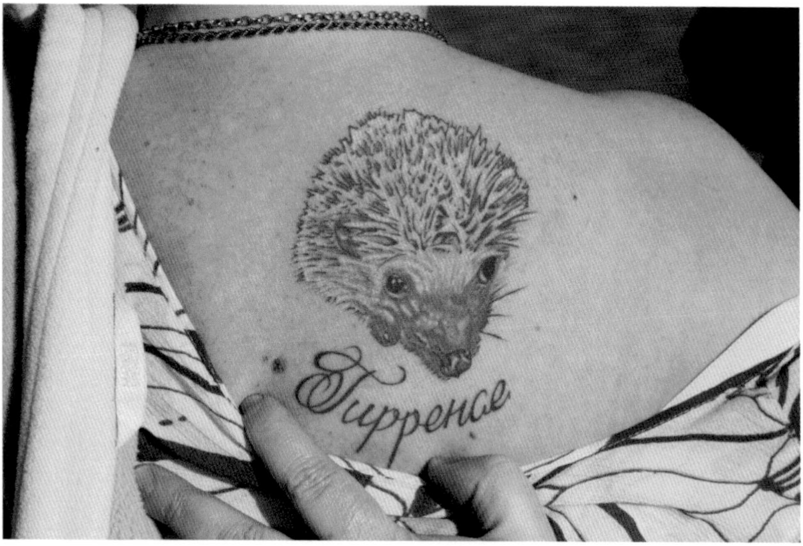

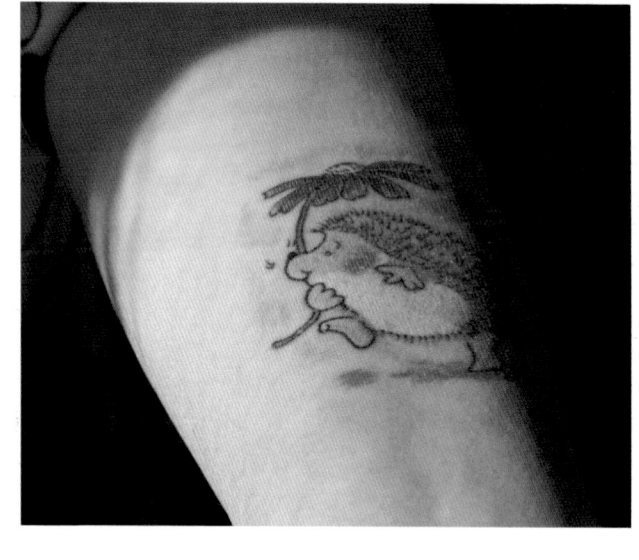

The affection people have for hedgehogs has manifest itself in many tattoos – some more lifelike than others.

Wild African pygmy hedgehogs, as these species, the African pygmy and Algerian, are sometimes known, come in a variety of colours, and this was something the breeders of the early domesticated animals were keen to exploit. Soon it became not just about getting pet hedgehogs, but about getting pet hedgehogs of each available colour and pattern. So developed has this trend become that in the Conformation Show there are very detailed guidelines as to what are considered to be acceptable characteristics.

To start with there is the seemingly simple matter of colour. There are now 92 colour varieties officially recognized, spread between two species: the white-bellied African pygmy hedgehog (*A. albiventris*) and the Algerian (*A. algirus*). Some of the dominant white-bellied hedgehog colours are Salt and Pepper, Dark Grey, Grey, Chocolate, Brown, Cinnamon, Ruby-eyed Cinnicot, Champagne, Apricot, Dark Cinnicot Snowflake, Albino and Pinto. The details are carefully described. For example, the Cinnamon hedgehog is defined thus:

Spines are white, banded by light cinnamon brown. No more than 5% of the spines are to be solid white. The face is not masked. The underbelly is white and mottling of the skin is not preferred. Skin on the shoulders is pink. The nose is liver.

Whereas,

Pinto is a colour pattern, rather than a colour and as such may appear on any coloured hedgehog. The Pinto pattern can be distinguished by a total lack of colour on the quills and skin beneath in distinct patches or spots over the hedgehog's back. Ideally, the white patches are to be symmetrical between one side of the hedgehog, divided down the length of the body by the dorsal, and the other. The remainder of the quills – those with coloured banding – remain consistent with the hedgehog's basic colouration.[3]

When the show begins, there are seven show classes: Pinto, Standard, Apricot, Snowflake, White, Albino and AOC (Any Other Colour). And if the colour conformation was not enough to contend with, hedgehogs are also judged on the form of their body shape. There, again, the rules are strict; the Standard of Perfection for African Pygmy Hedgehogs was revised in 1999:

> A standard of perfection can best be described as the ideal, or perfect goal that breeders attempt to see reflected in their animals. This standard should reflect the goals and desires of all breeders and hobbyists as they work to improve the quality and appearance of the animals they produce. The ultimate objective of this standard is to produce an ideal pet animal.

In the Official Booklet of Standards there even seems to be a hint of eugenics.

> Hedgehogs are cute, friendly and have an appeal that is truly unique. However, they do have certain physical characteristics that can be improved upon. As an example, being an insectivore, there is a natural tendency for them to have narrow heads and faces. By widening the head and shortening the face, the rest of the body will naturally follow. The animal's stance will widen . . . This will create a

far more attractive animal that should, theoretically, have the capacity to birth larger litters.

The points are awarded to each hedgehog while it is displayed on a stage by its human owner. The animal is encouraged to stand still while key elements are assessed. And while points are awarded for the form of the face, eyes, ears, colour and quills, it is temperament that takes the lion's share of points. Again, all the qualities are defined closely. A perfect face, for example, receives 5 per cent of the total score; to achieve even that, it must be

> wide and deep with the eyes spaced well apart. From above, the face shall proceed from the quill line to the nose in as straight a line as possible. From the side, the bridge of the nose shall proceed along an imaginary line to the top of the eye. The chin is to be deep and flow smoothly into the chest.

The 33 per cent awarded for temperament is split three ways: 11 per cent for the animal being unrolled; another 11 for flat quills; and a final 11 for personality. There is a deduction of 22 per cent for biting. For full marks to be achieved, the hedgehogs have to be very accustomed to being handled and being out in the day. The fact that so many of them are, though not all by any means, attests to their ability to be 'tamed'. Perhaps the pinnacle of prickly tameness comes from their ability to be coerced into performance, the basis of the International Hedgehog Olympic Games.

There have been occasions when people have thought this an elaborate joke, but the contestants at the Games, or at least their owners, take it very seriously. There are three events: the sprint, in which hedgehogs are placed in a large hamster ball which in turn is placed on plastic tracks (to ensure some direction to the run), and the time of the run is recorded; the hurdles, an event that requires the hedgehog to pass through a series of partitions in a length of cage – the partitions are raised from the floor, forcing a degree of climbing to take place; and last, the floor exercises: this is a more esoteric discipline with points being awarded to the hedgehog for walking through a tunnel, over a seesaw and, for a reason not fully explained, knocking over a My Little Pony model. Points are awarded for the style with which these tasks are completed and deducted for inappropriate defecation.

The excitement of the human combatants has to be tempered by the need to not frit the active participants, so flash photography and clapping are prohibited. However, waving of both hands above the head is taken as a sign of this reserved enthusiasm.

At the October 2007 show in Denver, Colorado, the winner of the games was a little hedgehog called Buttercup who was noticeable due to considerable scoliosis. She later went on to a career in education, featuring in a film for the National Scoliosis Foundation in the u.s., proving to the children it was aimed at that having a twisted spine did not prevent one from leading a normal and energetic life.

So is the hedgehog now a 'domestic' animal? Or is it still an exotic pet? And when does one become the other? The hedgehog does pretty well, meeting most of Diamond's defining features of domesticity: they have a capacity to be calm and unaggressive, able to be carried – at least before security checks increased – in the pockets of airline passengers without being noticed; they will remain relaxed and allow themselves to be petted; they certainly breed in captivity and are modified at the whim of the breeders; and while it is unclear what social hierarchies exist among wild

Others, like this one, are just simply very pretty (its name is Matilda, same as my daughter, so I might have been biased).

hedgehogs – most hedgehogs being solitary animals – their utility remains, at least until societal collapse, one of companionship (thereafter, I am sure they would become food again).

The community of hedgehog-keepers in the u.s. seems at times to have been split on what they were trying to achieve, with a minority under the impression that they were helping maintain stocks of wild African hedgehogs that were under threat of extinction in their homeland. It is fairly clear that the hedgehogs

The Rocky Mountain Hedgehog Show – trying to get the hedgehogs to stand still for judging is hard.

hitching a lift in the coat pockets of their owners, and exercising
on modified running wheels, would be unlikely to survive the
harsh realities of the wild.

This is not to say that domesticated hedgehogs don't have
needs; indeed there has been a flourishing cottage industry in
meeting them. The need for the hedgehogs to exercise was identified early on and quite some effort applied to developing a tool
to facilitate this. Traditional pet wheels did not work as the feet
of the hedgehog are considerably less dextrous than those of the
rodents for which they were designed, so hedgehog-specific
wheels were developed.

Other, less practical, needs are met, in some instances with quite dubious practice: for example, with the psychic investigation of a hedgehog's innermost thoughts. There is, apparently, a good business to be made as an animal communicator. And it seems that hedgehogs are a particularly good species to work with. In an article titled 'An Introduction to Animal Communication: Can We Really Talk to Hedgehogs?' Dawn Wrobel states,

> Animal communicators, animal intuitives and pet psychics are people who have developed the ability to communicate with animals in a conversational way. So, how does this work? I am clairaudient, so I actually hear the voice of the animal as if I were talking to another human. Most of this is telepathic – sent directly as mentally spoken thoughts to the animals and received back as spoken 'thoughts'. Other communicators might receive pictures or feelings rather than words.

The International Hedgehog Olympic Games has now been renamed the International Hedgehog Olympic Gymboree to avoid any confusion. The first of three disciplines is the sprint.

. . . How can this form of communication help you with your hedgehog? First, the process works by opening up two-way communication with your companion. Sometimes a problem is solved simply because the hedgehog has something he needs to get off his chest, and once he does, he is ok.[4]

On her website Wrobel explains a little more of how she works.

95% of sessions are completed by phone, so I first ask for the animal's name, age, breed and a picture or description. Since the animals and I work best in a question and answer format, I also ask that you provide 3–6 questions you would like to directly ask as a starting point for our conversation with your companion.

Floor exercises at the International Hedgehog Olympic Games.

And finally the hurdles at the International Hedgehog Olympic Games.

I begin each session by opening a telepathic connection with your animal companion. I receive messages in one of four ways: words, impressions, images or sensations.

And as a business model, it is good: there is no need to travel, and much opportunity to teach others the craft. The training on offer is structured such that to progress one must complete courses until such a point that one is able to take courses that allow you to teach the first course; and at this point, begin to recoup the initial investment.

This type of distant healing has been used on people with great effect – on the bank accounts of the 'healers', that is. Many bereaved pet owners gain comfort from knowing that their beloved hedgehog has passed over the Rainbow Bridge (the mythological bridge that some believe their pets cross and where they wait until they are reunited with their owners), but the fact that there is money to be made from misery should also ring alarm bells. The Rainbow Bridge has become an important focus for enthusiastic hedgehog owners and there is a special ceremony at the end of the Hedgehog Shows, at which all of the hedgehogs that have died in the intervening two years are celebrated with valedictions.

The impact that pet hedgehogs have on their owners is quite profound. The way that they are referred to should concern any human offspring expecting to see anything in the way of a bequest. These 'kids' are loved with a passion and intensity not seen in most human–animal relationships.

The spread of the craze around the rest of the world has been slower, but the hedgehog has become a feature of the exotic pet industry throughout much of Europe. As is the case with many other trends, there is a link with a child-friendly icon – in this case obviously Sonic the Hedgehog, though even Buttercup does not really match up to the whizz-bang excitement of the little blue hog.

Every now and then someone tries to stimulate the market in Britain. There have regularly been stories in the media featuring the latest, cutest photographs of baby hedgehogs. The breeders maintain that they are acting responsibly and that they are surprised when the pictures appear all over the media. But that could be seen as a little disingenuous, as the release of the pictures only ever coincides with a litter in search of buyers.

Sitting in a box of chocolates or an egg cup are the usual clichés. And there is no denying the cuteness. But campaigners in Britain have been calling for a halt to this particular experiment. While the breeders in the papers may well be reputable and well-meaning, there will always be a chancer out there who will try collecting European hedgehogs and selling them on. Additionally, the host of hedgehog carers around the country have a hard enough time as it is keeping up with the arrivals of native hedgehogs. The inevitable influx of African pygmy hedgehogs when owners get bored – as they tend to with fad pets – would add a great strain with the additional problem that, unlike the local species, these ones could not be released into the wild. There is no way we can affect the fascination people have with exotic pets; it is just important to have an articulate response in the hope that we can prevent the rise of a new fad pet.

9 Helping Hedgehogs

More than any other wild animal on the planet, the hedgehog lends itself to being cared for by people. This is down to two, or arguably three, key characteristics. First, they tend to live as natural neighbours, inhabiting suburban gardens and being unmissable when seen. Second, they tolerate attention. A hedgehog's reaction to human presence and intervention is unlike most other species; they do not run and they do not attack. They are by nature defensive, and this tendency allows initial contact between themselves and other species. And many hedgehogs, when they have become accustomed to contact, will then allow fairly intimate examination and, if needed, medical care. Third, they are, in part because of these other two characteristics, much loved.

There is much about the behaviour of a wild hedgehog that is, in effect, like that of a domesticated animal. Most wild mammals will run from a human or, if unable to take flight, will fight. In fact this description could be extended to include most vertebrates. And so, while many vertebrates are quite accessible, few offer the same sort of connection as is often possible with a hedgehog.

Additionally, apart from the 'cute' nature of their face, if a hedgehog is not rolled in a ball, it will look up. It is rare to be looked down upon by a hedgehog. And the process of looking up

puts the animal in a vulnerable position, with the neck becoming exposed; many people find such vulnerability attractive. In many ways, the adult, wild hedgehog behaves like a proto-pet, as if it was already partially domesticated, and this is part of the delight; there is an accessible connection with the wild through each hedgehog.

Hedgehog care comes, broadly, in two forms: care for the individual and care for the population as a whole.

Hedgehogs seen out in the daytime are often ill; this one is being a 'stunt' hedgehog for a photo shoot and was returned to its carer after I was finished.

HEDGEHOG HOSPITALS

Although folk tales featuring hedgehogs, or hedgehog/baby changelings, would suggest that it was not unusual to have a

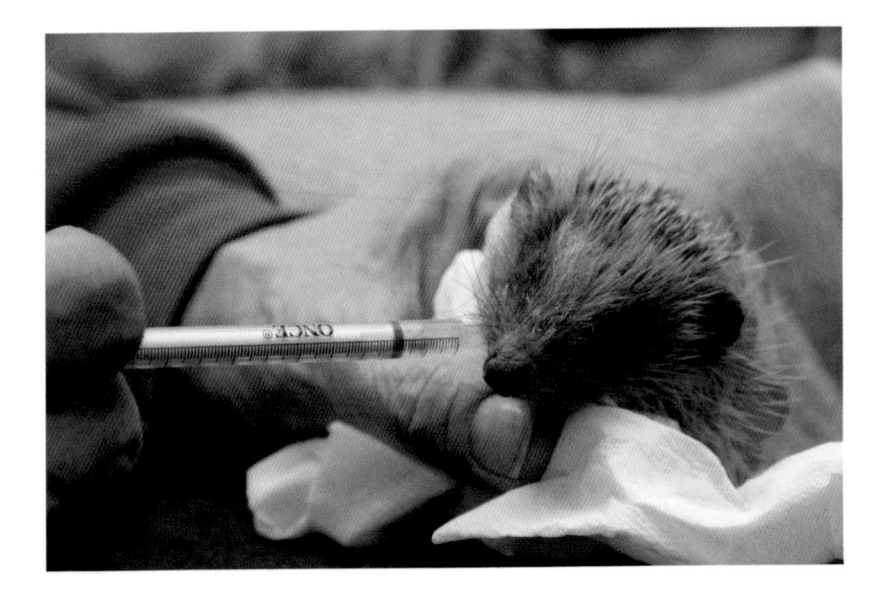

Hedgehog carers frequently go to great lengths to resuscitate sick or injured hedgehogs. Here Elaine Drewrey from Hedgehog Care in Authorpe feeds an adolescent.

hedgehog in the home, there are no records of early hedgehog care. There are currently wildlife hospitals throughout Europe, but what is fascinating is the concentration of single-species wildlife hospitals that cater solely for hedgehogs. The number of such hospitals in Britain alone is extraordinary: the British Hedgehog Preservation Society has a list of over 600 hedgehog carers, and this is by no means comprehensive.

Hedgehog carers in Britain are split into two camps. There are the hospitals that take in pretty much all native wildlife; some are extremely well-funded and most are usually well-equipped. The best-known of them is probably the Wildlife Hospital Trust, marketed as St Tiggywinkles, where animals can expect the attentions of some surprising carers; it is not unusual, for example, to find a badger receiving root-canal surgery from a Harley Street dental surgeon.

And then there is the other style of carer: usually working alone, they care for just hedgehogs, and they are usually women. Within this community the amount of involvement can vary considerably. Some rarely move on from the occasional cardboard box in the kitchen, the route by which most people who enter this world are initially hooked. It is no accident that Les Stocker, founder of St Tiggywinkles, called one of his books *Something in a Cardboard Box* (1989).

So why is there such a focus on hedgehog care? Because of the three points above: they are nearby, friendly and attractive. Hedgehogs are more likely than other animals to be found in a parlous state due to their ability to cope with living in close proximity to people. It is likely, on the other hand, that the vast majority of ill or injured rural hedgehogs receive little or no attention, simply because they are not seen. Second, hedgehogs

While hedgehogs tend to arrive at hedgehog hospitals in cardboard boxes, they often end up in bowls and other receptacles.

'allow' intervention by dint of their behaviour; most other animals would require an experienced wildlife carer simply to control and contain them, but hedgehogs do all that themselves. And finally, hedgehogs are appealing; people are drawn to them as much by their actual appearance as by the aura of benignity that surrounds them. It does them no harm either that they have been considered, since 1905 and Beatrix Potter's public relations campaign, to be one of the 'good guys'.

Over the years the quality of care on offer to hedgehogs has increased dramatically as the community of carers, with varying degrees of success, have shared their experiences with one another. This has happened formally through books and courses and also through a far more informal network of self-supporting independent carers. This knowledge exchange has been greatly assisted by the advent of social media, where questions about a new patient can be quickly passed among hundreds of other carers. Corners of Facebook will sometimes come alive to the debates surrounding a photograph, not of a cute kitten, but of the parasitic worms found in a sample of hedgehog faeces.

The basics of hedgehog care are easy to pick up if you are willing to dedicate time to your charges, and many of the more established carers have a host of satellite carers who take on the hedgehogs that need less demanding care. Many hedgehogs can be helped simply with warmth, fluid and food. But when it comes to more complex problems, what has been learned over the years now means that hedgehogs have a great chance of surviving. Frequently the problems are down to the time of birth: if too late in the year, the hedgehog will find that the weather is getting colder and food is therefore harder to obtain, so a cycle of decline can set in, manifesting itself in hypothermia. The animals are also prone, when run down like this, to parasitic infections such as lungworm. The best starting point for a novice carer is the website of the British Hedgehog Preservation Society; for a more detailed introduction, Kay Bullen has written a guide called *Hedgehog Rehabilitation*.

One widespread exercise to try to help hedgehogs made it into every available media: the campaign to halt the cull of hedgehogs on the Outer Hebridean islands called the Uists. The unfortunate hedgehogs there had been imported to the previously prickle-free islands in the 1970s; by the 1990s their presence was being linked to the decline in breeding success of ground-nesting birds. Original plans to export the hedgehogs alive were dismissed and a cull ensued. Given the strength of feeling generally evident towards hedgehogs, it is unsurprising that there was some vociferous protest and, after four years and a research project proving the error of one of the key assumptions that led to the proposed cull, the project shifted back to removing the animals alive and releasing them on mainland Scotland.[1]

HEDGEHOG CONSERVATION

It is tragic that one of the most effective ways of assessing fluctuations in the population of hedgehogs is by counting those encountered dead on the roads, though the results are read in a way that one might not perhaps expect. Indeed, it is slightly counter-intuitive, but one actually feels a sense of glee when more dead hedgehogs are seen, as this indicates that the overall population numbers are higher. Clearly this measure will not provide an absolute number, but it does allow, if repeated year after year, an assessment to be made of the direction in which the population is moving.

The assumption that more dead hedgehogs represents more in the wild only holds true if the occasionally postulated idea that hedgehogs are evolving mechanisms to avoid being run over is not true. Unfortunately there is no evidence to support the idea that hedgehogs are becoming smarter at dealing with cars. The defence mechanism that is so helpful in allowing people to rescue hedgehogs is obviously less effective when a hedgehog is confronted by a vehicle. The idea was mooted that hedgehogs that ran would live to breed and therefore pass on the running response to danger genetically. But would running necessarily increase the chances of survival of a hedgehog? Probably not; a hedgehog could just as easily be running from safety to danger, as in the opposite direction.

The problem for hedgehogs is not just that they get killed on the roads, but that roads fragment their habitat. This is at the heart of the problem of population decline. Recent research has shown that the population of hedgehogs in Britain fell by 37 per cent in suburbia between 2003 and 2012.[2] This terrible scale of decline is why the hedgehog, still considered widespread and common by many people, has been placed on the Priority List of the Biodiversity Action Plan. Indeed, the decline could be even worse. A population estimate for hedgehogs in Britain from 1950 was about 30 million. The estimate now is less than 1.5 million. That is a 95 per cent decline. Even if the 1950 figure happened to be a drastic overestimate – for example, if the population was actually half that number – this would still reveal a decline of 90 per cent.

Perhaps these are the reasons behind a recent upsurge in concern for the hedgehog. And while claims from some researchers that we are facing the imminent extinction of this much loved creature are wrong, there is certainly going to come a time, soon, when the reassuring snuffle of the hedgehog in the garden will become a rarity. So why has there been such a problem for hedgehogs?

Ecology rarely presents easy answers to simple questions, and this is a case in point. We can simplify the problem a lot to loss of habitat and habitat fragmentation; it is just that within those descriptors there is a great deal of detail. Hedgehogs are woodland-edge specialists; furthermore, the human creation of hedges leads to a great expansion of potential hedgehog

The hedgehogs in New Zealand are not immune to the power of the car tyre. The brilliant Burton Silver invented some retaliation.

habitat. It is possible that hedgehog numbers flourished with the rise of agriculture, the hedgerow being a good approximation of the edge of a woodland.

Following the end of the Second World War, the dramatic increase in the mechanization of agriculture led to an equally dramatic loss of hedgerows. While the grubbing up of hedges no longer receives financial motivation in the form of subsidies designed to encourage field size expansion, there has simultaneously been such a stripping of people from the countryside that there are few people left willing or able to manage hedges to the benefit of hedgehogs and other wildlife. And while this is a serious impediment to the progress of the hedgehog throughout the rural landscape, it is but one of a number of problems facing the animal.

As farming has intensified, so the macro-invertebrate fauna of the fields has diminished. The worms, beetles and larvae on which the hedgehog feeds need a diverse environment to survive. In the last century, however, 97 per cent of wildflower meadows have been destroyed in Britain, many in favour of crops of rye grass for silage. The hedgehog food has gone.[3]

And just as hedgehog food has gone, so too has the shelter on which they rely. A study in the Netherlands found that 75 per cent of hedgehog breeding nests were sited within hedgerows, as were nearly 50 per cent of hibernation nesting sites (the rest being made up of woodland and, to a small extent, anthropogenic structures) and 60 per cent of day-nests (a further 20 per cent of day nests were sited in woodland). In total, hedgehogs were found to spend around 55 per cent of their time either within a hedgerow or within a 5-metre-wide zone on either side.[4]

England and Wales lost hedges at a rate of 18,000 km per year in the 1990s, a process which is continuing. This has often been through poor management, resulting in what were once hedges being reclassified as 'tree lines' or 'gappy shrubs'. And while those landscape features retain some value for wildlife, for hedgehogs they are less useful; not just because they are indicative of a management style that results in lower macro-invertebrate fauna in the soil, but also because they provide less shelter.

As a woodland-edge specialist, hedgehogs will gravitate towards shelter. This is because, while they have a fantastic defence against most potential predators with their spines, there is one animal that trundles the same territory that can, and will, feast on the little urchins. This creates something of a quandary for conservationists, because a big effort was put into protecting the badger, and now the badger is having a serious impact on the ability of the hedgehog to thrive. There have been quite heated discussions, with the badger fans feeling not a little defensive. Not only are badgers facing an onslaught from the dairy industry, which is desperately floundering around trying to identify an excuse for the inevitable results of farmers' intensification of production, and finding the badger the perfect scapegoat for bovine tuberculosis, but hedgehog ecologists have mapped the distribution of hedgehogs and badgers, finding that in most instances, where there are more than thirteen badgers within an area of 10 square kilometres, hedgehogs are under serious threat of localized extinction.

This is because, while the spines of a hedgehog are long enough to protect them against many predators, the claws of a badger are longer. So a badger acquainted with the taste of hedgehog – and there does seem to be some learning required – can open up a tightly rolled hedgehog and feast.

Predation is not the only threat posed by the badger to the hedgehog; badgers and hedgehogs consume the same food – macro-invertebrates – with an emphasis on worms in both cases. As hedgehog expert Pat Morris says, 'the same worm cannot be eaten by both.'[5] This competitive relationship weighs heavily in favour of the badger, which is able to consume around seven times the volume of worms a hedgehog can manage.

The result is a complex 'asymmetric intraguild predatory relationship', which is in itself fascinating.[6] The two species compete for the same food resource, hence are in the same ecological guild. But when the situation changes – perhaps with food resources becoming more scarce – the relationship changes from being competitive (in the badgers' favour) to being predatory (again in the badgers' favour). This is a similar relationship as between lions and hyenas; while they at first compete for the same food, it can all change to being predatory if pressures in the environment increase.

The complex relationship between badgers and hedgehogs extends still further. The problem for hedgehogs is not that they all get eaten by badgers, but that the presence of badgers amplifies the most important constraint on a healthy hedgehog population; badgers further fragment the environment, achieving this at times by scent alone, as was revealed by a delightfully idiosyncratic piece of research at Oxford University. To conduct the experiment, three varieties of water-bomb-like vessels were prepared:

> We made odour missiles from blown, oven-dried quail eggs refilled with dissolved (one part faeces to one part water) badger, fruit bat or sheep faeces . . . After the first observation period an egg was selected at random and thrown to within approximately 0.3 m of the hedgehog. On impact, the eggs nearly always smashed open liberating the odour . . . the hedgehog's behaviour was observed for the second period. At the end of this period the egg was inspected to determine the type of odour . . .[7]

The result of this was that the hedgehogs reacted most strongly to the explosion of badger scent by dramatically altering their course, indicating that badger activity will inhibit the ability of hedgehogs to use the same space. And as we have already seen, hedgehogs also have a very strong inclination to remain in or near hedgerows; thus badger activity in hedgerows will have a substantial impact on hedgehogs' ability to move through a landscape, because badger scent sends hedgehogs back to where they came from, preventing dispersal.

These results clearly indicate how the presence of badgers adds to the fragmentation of the habitat, a problem more usually associated with infrastructural development, most obviously roads; people often see hedgehogs squashed on the road more frequently than they see them live in their gardens. And it is true that hedgehogs are very vulnerable to traffic; indeed, many a cartoon has taken as its theme either the demise or the revenge of the hedgehog.

As mentioned, road casualties are a useful tool for assessing population fluctuations. A research project established by the People's Trust for Endangered Species, Mammals on Roads, now has its own smartphone app to help in the collection of data. And so, while an increase in dead hedgehogs might seem like a bad sign, it does actually indicate an increase in the population in the surrounding area.

However, the biggest problem presented by roads is that when the traffic on them increases beyond an as-yet-undetermined level, the roads become insurmountable obstacles. Indeed, hedgehogs do not even attempt to cross big roads.[8] Sometimes, and increasingly, this is no longer dependent on the numbers of cars as, for safety reasons, continuous concrete barriers are placed along the middle of great lengths of dual carriageway and motorway.

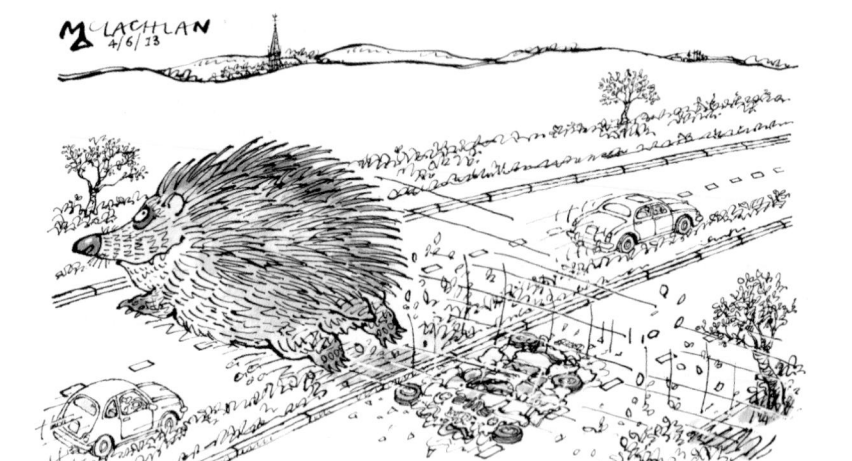

The artist's signature reads "McLACHLAN 4/6/13"

Sometimes the revenge of the hedgehog comes in a more dramatic form.

Habitat fragmentation is bad for hedgehogs as it creates pockets of hedgehog habitat that cannot operate as part of a whole. Each little island is then susceptible to piecemeal extinction, and unable to be replenished should the population fall to dangerous levels. The most recent research from Oxford University has revealed quite the scale of the problem. Computer modelling has shown that the minimum viable population that will sustain hedgehogs in an area is 32, and that the minimum area in suburbia must be at least 90 ha – the equivalent of at least two 18-hole golf courses, unfragmented. These are becoming a rare commodity.[9]

Habitat fragmentation can also be less obvious. With the rural landscape frequently turned into a desert by intensive farming, filled with hungry badgers, the tranquillity of suburbia has become an effective refuge. Again, the capacity of the hedgehog to tolerate humanity in its more benign form comes in handy. However, the way in which we manage our suburbs has been changing. Increased traffic is creating smaller islands of safety. And within these islands – usually accumulations of gardens or municipal parks – there are threats too. A person may create the most hedgehog-friendly environment, but it may still be to no avail: there may be a compost heap, rich in rotting vegetation and complete with all the hedgehog food this brings; there may be a pond fitted with an escape ramp or beach (because while hedgehogs can swim, they cannot swim forever and need to get out of whatever water they get into); there may be a garden-wide injunction on agrichemicals like slug pellets, which would be good because the accumulative and sub-lethal effects of these chemicals is unknown and because hedgehogs like to eat slugs, and not all slugs are evil – some are important contributors to a healthy garden; and there may be a rough patch of brambles in a corner that is always left as a structure under which hedgehogs may build a home. But all of this is irrelevant if the garden is bounded by a hedgehog-proof fence.

Despite the cartoons, hedgehogs do still end up two-dimensional which, while being sad for the individual, also presents a very useful technique for monitoring fluctuations in overall population

Even when the road is free from traffic, it can still present an impenetrable barrier if fitted with miles of concrete wall.

A hedgehog will often roam across many gardens in a single night. They can easily cover over a kilometre in that time and will be seeking a diverse collection of environments to meet their needs: food, shelter, water and, at the right time of year, potential mates. To facilitate this the People's Trust for Endangered Species and the British Hedgehog Preservation Society collaborated to create Hedgehog Street in 2011, a campaign to encourage communities to look beyond the hedgehog-friendliness of their individual gardens and see how they can work together to make a more useful, larger area for hedgehogs.

And while the focus is on hedgehogs, it is inevitable that when people make moves to improve things for one species, they will, often inadvertently, be improving the environment for a whole host of other species. This is why the iconic status of the hedgehog is so valuable. The hedgehog is, as we have seen, a species with which people can quickly feel some kinship. But unlike the sentimental fondness many may feel for the charismatic megafauna such as lions, tigers, elephants and whales, where any efforts to personally help preserve them from extinction are so very remote, the act of helping improve a garden for a hedgehog is something tangible, and has far-reaching consequences.

The British media's reaction to Hedgehog Street was, again, indicative of the attraction of the animal; with stories appearing in most newspapers, and television stations picking up the story too, thousands of households around the country took up the challenge to improve their own space and link it with their neighbours'.

The linking simply required at least that people ensured there were hedgehog-sized spaces for the animals to trundle through. But there were suggestions for more radical moves as well. One of the great losses of suburbia has been the increase in low-maintenance gardening options; decking, patios and extensions have swamped what were once semi-wild spaces. Front gardens have suffered too, many being turned into parking spots. People were asked to consider opening up their gardens a little more, sacrificing a little convenience for the greater good of hedgehog happiness.

Working with people's enthusiasm, Hedgehog Street also created a virtual community of people sharing their top tips for

Hedgehogs are carnivores; they should not be fed bread and milk. And while regular meaty pet food is fine, you can now obtain carefully formulated and taste-tested hedgehog food.

hedgehog salvation, posting photographs of what they had achieved. Is there any other garden animal that could so effectively encourage such radical action in the gardens of suburbia? The fondness for the animal is clearly not new. For years people have been putting food out for hedgehogs. Until the 1980s, when hedgehog carers began to take note of the well-being of the animals, the staple was often bread and milk (which is not great for hedgehogs as they do not digest lactose well). Now there are specific hedgehog foods available, made from a carefully selected mix that will meet the needs of the animal.

The invention of Spike's Dinner was strangely topsy-turvy, with the bank manager of a Lincolnshire pet shop – who had just rescued a hedgehog – asking his client if there was any particular food he should give to the animal; clearly the usual route is for the pet shop to approach the bank manager. Marion Horscraft, owner of the pet shop, started to ask hedgehog carers and found that a high-meat, chicken-based food seemed to be preferred. But that still did not answer the question of what was best. My children will eat sweets until they are sick; it is not always good to rely on preference when assessing the most beneficial diet!

Marion developed a variety of food that met the needs of the hedgehog – including extra taurine – with four different formulations tested at hedgehog hospitals before Spike's Dinner was born. The design of the label emerged from a late-night sketching session by hedgehog carer Elaine Drewery before the reality dawned that to start the business, they would have to commit to the creation of 20 tonnes of food: a run of 250,000 cans. Would anyone be interested?

Again the passion people have for the hedgehog revealed itself. Marion ended up doing over 40 live radio interviews, appearing on three television programmes and in most of the printed press as well. Recently rebranded as Spike's Hedgehog Food, there is now a range of options available with which to tempt your spiky visitors. There are also ingenious solutions to the issue of getting the food to the hedgehog, and not the cat, rat or fox, with clever designs of feeding stations published online to download.[10]

Of course, with the increased human involvement has come a new worry: does putting food out for hedgehogs make them dependent? Will a holiday away from home result in starving hedgehogs? The simple answer is no. Hedgehogs are delightfully promiscuous. There is a famous children's story by Inga Moore, *Six Dinner Sid*, about a cat who is found to be 'owned' by six different households, each of which is feeding him. Hedgehogs are a little like that. Remember the distance they can travel at night, should the fences allow; this also means that the person who thinks that 'their' hedgehog comes to 'their' garden every night to feed might well not be just 'their' hedgehog. Additionally, that 'one' hedgehog that keeps coming back might in fact be many.

Pat Morris undertook a study looking at this and found that over seventeen nights, at least eleven different animals visited her principal food bowl. If you are feeling proprietorial about the hedgehog in your garden and willing to risk the truth, next time you see it, pop a spot of nail varnish or correction fluid on a few spines (being careful not to let it touch the skin). This should last a few weeks, so you will be able to tell if the marked hedgehog, alone, returns. And if you are feeling like learning a little more, develop a simple system: a mark on its top left for the first, on the top right for a second animal, and so on. You will then be able to build a picture of the comings and goings of your hedgehog(s).

All this care, love and attention given to the practical well-being of the hedgehog is clearly informed by the vast collection of folk and cultural references. Most people do not have the good fortune to meet with hedgehogs regularly, yet most feel a great deal of compassion towards this unlikely animal. They are deeply rooted in our psyches now as a gentle and somewhat humorous component of the ecosystem. There is a lot more for us to learn about hedgehogs, and there is also a lot for us to learn from hedgehogs. They are very special. Unique in their approachability, there is no other animal so easy to get nose-to-nose with and see some of the glint of the wild.

Timeline of the Hedgehog

Earliest records of Eulipotyphla; mammals with a basic form not massively dissimilar to modern-day relatives

Fossils dating from the Eocene can be directly linked to our modern-day hedgehogs

Deinogalerix, the 'terrible shrew', a dog-sized hedgehog that used to live in what is now southern Italy

The ancient Greek warrior-poet Archilochus declares that 'The fox knows many thing, but the hedgehog knows one big thing.'

Pliny the Elder writes his *Natural History*, containing many of the myths about hedgehogs that will last until modern times

Beatrix Potter publishes *The Tale of Mrs Tiggy-Winkle*, stimulating a change in the way people look at the hedgehog

The foundation of the British Hedgehog Preservation Society (BHPS), sparked by the discovery of hedgehogs dead in cattle grids; getting ramps installed in cattle grids is its first campaign

Sonic the Hedgehog is launched for the Sega Mega Drive. The blue hedgehog becomes one of the most iconic computer game characters of all time

End of the last ice age
saw the arrival of two
new species of hedgehog
to Europe

Sumerians and ancient Egyptians
creating amulets and other
ornamentation in the shape
of hedgehogs

Late Bronze Age child found
buried at Stonehenge with
what looks like a small chalk
hedgehog

The chapel at New College,
Oxford, is founded, and features
a startlingly pagan array of
misericords, including two
hedgehogs

Arthur Schopenhauer publishes
Parerga and Paralipomena, in
which he posits the 'hedgehog's
dilemma'

Lewis Carroll invents a version
of croquet featuring hedgehogs
as balls. The game proves difficult

A cull of hedgehogs
begins on the Uists in
the Outer Hebrides,
sparking a UK-wide
campaign that succeeds
in getting it halted in
2007

'The State of Britain's Hedgehogs'
report published by the People's
Trust for Endangered Species and
the BHPS. It reveals the startling
news that the population has
declined by, at the very least,
25 per cent in the previous ten
years. There is some evidence to
suggest the decline could be up
to 95 per cent in the last 60 years

References

1 WHAT IS A HEDGEHOG?

1 Nigel Reeve, *Hedgehogs* (London 1994), pp. 37–40.
2 Ibid., p. 2.
3 G. B. Corbet, 'The Family Erinaceidae: A Synthesis of its Taxonomy, Phylogeny, Ecology and Zoogeography', *Mammal Review*, 18 (1988), pp. 117–72.
4 Walter Poduschka and Christl Poduschka, 'Kreuzungsversuche an mitteleuropaischen Igeln', *Säugetierkundliche Mitteilungen*, 31 (1983), pp. 1–12.
5 Reeve, *Hedgehogs*, p. 18.
6 Pat Morris, *The New Hedgehog Book* (Stansted, 2006), pp. 24–6.
7 T.H.V. Rich, 'Origin and History of the Erinaceinae and Brachyericinae (Mammalia, Insectivora) in North America', *Bulletin of the American Museum of Natural History*, CLXXI/1 (1981).
8 J. M Seddon et al., 'DNA Footprints of European Hedgehogs, *Erinaceus europaeus* and *E. concolor*: Pleistocene Refugia, Postglacial Expansion and Colonization Routes', *Molecular Ecology*, X/9 (2001), pp. 2187–98.
9 Jim Giles, 'Could Astronauts Sleep their Way to the Stars?', *Nature*, www.nature.com, 3 August 2004.
10 Morris, *New Hedgehog Book*, pp. 139–46.
11 Penny Rimbaud, interview with the author, March 2006.
12 Morris, *New Hedgehog Book*, pp. 57–61.
13 Kathleen Adams, Letters to the Editor, *The Times* (21 January 1933).
14 'Shameless Mammals: Horny Hedgehogs Spark Police Callout',

Der Spiegel Online, www.spiegel.de/international, 25 July 2007.
15 Morris, *New Hedgehog Book*, p. 8.

2 HEDGEHOG NAMES AND FOLKLORE

1 Hartwig Altenmüller, 'Funerary Boats and Boat Pits of the Old Kingdom', *Quarterly Journal of African and Asian Studies*, LXX/3 (2002), pp. 269–90.
2 Magda van Ryneveld, 'Hedgehogs in Ancient Egyptian Art', *Ancient Egypt*, XXXVII/1 (2006), pp. 17–19.
3 Donald B. Redford, ed., *The Oxford Encyclopedia of Ancient Egypt* (New York, 2001).
4 Béla Gunda, 'Gypsy Medical Folklore in Hungary', *Journal of American Folklore*, LXXV/296 (April–June 1962), pp. 131–46.
5 Marija Gimbutas, *The Goddesses and Gods of Old Europe, 6500–3500 BC: Myths and Cult Images* (Berkeley, CA, 1974), pp. 179–81.
6 Li Wei-tsu, 'On the Cult of the Four Sacred Animals in the Neighbourhood of Peking', *Folklore Studies*, VII (1948), pp. 1–94.
7 C. Gardner, 'Folk-lore in Mongolia', *The Folk-lore Journal*, III/4 (1885), pp. 312–28.
8 David A. Leeming, *Creation Myths of the World: An Encyclopedia*, 2nd edn (Santa Barbara, CA, 2010), pp. 233–4.
9 Pliny the Elder, *The Natural History*, trans. John Bostock (London, 1855), Book 8, chapter 56.
10 Isidore of Seville, *Etymologies* [7th century], Book 12, section 3, para. 7.
11 Pat Morris, *The New Hedgehog Book* (Stansted, 2006), p. 181.
12 Christopher Kleinhenz, ed., *Medieval Italy: An Encyclopedia*, vol. I (New York, 2004).
13 Roger Lovegrove, *Silent Fields: The Long Decline of a Nation's Wildlife* (Oxford, 2007), pp. 186–91.
14 John Clare, *Selected Poetry* (London, 1990), p. 119.
15 Hugh Warwick, *A Prickly Affair: The Charm of the Hedgehog* (London, 2008), p. 248.

16 John Mason Neale, *Mediaeval Preachers and Mediaeval Preaching . . .* (London, 1856), pp. 246–7.

17 Moses Gaster, *Rumanian Bird and Beast Stories* (London, 1915).

18 Johann Georg von Hahn, *Griechische und albanesische Märchen* (Leipzig, 1864), vol. II, story no. 91, pp. 103–4, trans. D. L. Ashliman 2011, at www.pitt.edu/~dash/ashliman.html, accessed 12 December 2013.

19 E. M. Leather, 'Scraps of English Folklore XIV (Herefordshire, Worcestershire, Middlesex, and Monmouthshire)', *Folklore*, XXXVII/3 (September 1926), pp. 296–8.

20 Linda Garrity, *Fabulous Fables: Using Fables with Children Grades Two to Four* (Glenview, IL, 1991), p. 39.

21 Steven Morris, 'Bat or Badger? It's the Roadkill Recipe Book', *Guardian* (31 January 2006).

3 HISTORICAL HEDGEHOGS

1 Ernst Mayr, *The Growth of Biological Thought* (Cambridge, MA, 1981), p. 330.

2 'Destroyers: U Class 1943: *Urchin* (1943)', www.britainsnavy.co.uk, 3 July 2012.

4 LITERARY HEDGEHOGS

1 Walter Gregor, 'Some Folk-lore on Trees, Animals, and River-fishing, from the North-east of Scotland', *The Folk-lore Journal*, VII/1 (1889), pp. 41–4.

2 Wilhelm Grimm and Jacob Grimm, *Hans the Hedgehog*, trans. Margaret Taylor (1884), at www.classiclit.about.com, accessed 6 December 2013.

3 Charles Godfrey Leland, 'Aldegonda, The Fairy of Joy: An Italian Tale', *Journal of American Folklore*, VI/22 (July–September 1893), pp. 228–31.

4 Lewis Carroll, *Alice's Adventures in Wonderland and Through the Looking-Glass and What Alice Found There* (Oxford, 1998), pp. 73–4.

5 Tom Wakeford, *Liaisons of Life: From Hornworts to Hippos, How the Unassuming Microbe Has Driven Evolution* (Chichester, 2001), p. 21.
6 Gerald Durrell, *Birds, Beasts and Relatives* (London, 1976).
7 Gordon D. Griffiths, *Mattie: The Story of a Hedgehog* (London, 1967).
8 Johann Christian Polycarp Erxleben, *Elementary Principles of Natural History* [1782], quoted in Walter and Christl Podushka, *Dearest Prickles: The Story of a Hegdehog Family* (London, 1972).
9 Ted Hughes, *Letters of Ted Hughes*, ed. Christopher Reid (London, 2007), pp. 10–11.

5 PHILOSOPHICAL HEDGEHOGS

1 Isaiah Berlin, *The Hedgehog and the Fox: An Essay on Tolstoy's View of History* (London, 1953), pp. 3–4.
2 Arianna Huffington, 'Why America is Deeply in Need of a Good Hedgehog', *Huffington Post*, www.huffingtonpost.com, 17 August 2011.
3 http://blogs.p2pu.org/neurobiolaw/2009/09/15/hedgehogs-aristotle-and-ritalin, accessed March 2013, no longer available.
4 Ronald Dworkin, *Justice for Hedgehogs* (Cambridge, MA, 2011), pp. 1, 419–22.
5 Nicholas Wade, Marco Piccolino and Adrian Simmons, 'Arthur Schopenhauer', *Portraits of European Neuroscientists*, www.neuroportraits.eu, accessed 8 December 2013.

6 ARTISTIC HEDGEHOGS

1 Ron Jeremy, *Ron Jeremy: The Hardest (Working) Man in Showbiz* (New York, 2007), pp. 67–70.
2 Hugh Warwick, *A Prickly Affair: The Charm of the Hedgehog* (London, 2008), p. 163.
3 Personal communication with the author, 11 November 2011.

7 COMMERCIAL HEDGEHOGS

1 Barbara J. Phillips, 'Advertising and the Cultural Meaning of Animals', *Advances in Consumer Research*, XXIII (1996), pp. 354–60.
2 Ibid.

8 DOMESTIC HEDGEHOGS

1 J. G. Wood, *Petland Revisited* (London, 1903), Preface, p. vii.
2 Naomi Wikane, 'Whence the Hedgehog', *The Hedgehog Welfare Society Newsletter*, IX (March 2004), p. 9, at www.hedgehogwelfare.org.
3 The International Hedgehog Association, 'Understanding Colors: Color Guide' (2012), at www.hedgehogclub.com.
4 Dawn Wrobel, 'An Introduction to Animal Communication: Can We Really Talk to Hedgehogs?', *IHA News* (September–October 2008).

9 HELPING HEDGEHOGS

1 Hugh Warwick et al., 'Survival and Weight Changes of Hedgehogs Translocated from the Hebrides to Mainland Scotland', *Lutra*, XLIX/2 (2006), pp. 89–102.
2 People's Trust for Endangered Species, 'Hegdehog Decline and 10 Year Analysis' (January 2013), press release, www.ptes.org.
3 R. M. Fuller, 'The Changing Extent and Conservation Interest of Lowland Grasslands in England and Wales: A Review of Grassland Surveys, 1930–84', *Biological Conservation*, XL (1987), pp. 281–300.
4 Marcel Huijser, 'Life on the Edge: Hedgehog Traffic Victims and Mitigation Strategies in an Anthropogenic Landscape', PhD thesis, Wageningen University (2000).
5 Pat Morris, *The New Hedgehog Book* (Stansted, 2006), pp. 159–61.
6 C. P. Doncaster, 'Testing the Role of Intraguild Predation in Regulating Hedgehog Populations', *Proceedings of the Royal Society: Biological Sciences*, CCXLIX/1324 (July 1992), pp. 113–17.

7 J. F. Ward, 'Hedgehog Response to Badger Odour', *Animal Behaviour*, LIII/4 (1997), pp. 709–12.

8 C. Rondinni et al., 'Roads as Barriers to Movement for Hedgehogs', *Functional Ecology*, XVI (2002), pp. 504–9.

9 People's Trust for Endangered Species, 'Hedgehog Minimum Viable Population Report' (November 2013), press release, www.ptes.org.

10 Epping Forest Hedgehog Rescue, 'How to Prevent Other Animals Like Dogs, Cats or Foxes Stealing the Hedgehog's Food', www.thehedgehog.co.uk, accessed 6 December 2013.

Select Bibliography

Berlin, Isaiah, *The Hedgehog and the Fox: An Essay on Tolstoy's View of History* (London, 1953)

British Hedgehog Preservation Society, *Prickly Poems: An Anthology of Hedgehog Poems* (London, 1992)

Bullen, K., *Hedgehog Rehabilitation* (Ludlow, 2002)

Burton, M., *The Hedgehog* (London, 1969)

Carroll, Lewis, *Alice's Adventures in Wonderland and Through the Looking-Glass and What Alice Found There* (Oxford, 1998)

Clare, John, *Selected Poetry* (London, 1990)

Dworkin, Ronald, *Justice for Hedgehogs* (Cambridge, MA, 2011)

Harris, Stevie, and Derek Yalden, *Mammals of the British Isles* (Southampton, 2008)

Lovegrove, Roger, *Silent Fields: The Long Decline of a Nation's Wildlife* (Oxford, 2007)

Macdonald, David, ed., *The Encyclopedia of Mammals* (Oxford, 2009)

Mayers, Richard, *Spikez: Half Hedgehog, Half Machine. All Prickles* (St Albans, 2012)

Morris, Pat, *The New Hedgehog Book* (Stansted, 2006)

Poduschka, W., and C. Poduschka, *Dearest Prickles: The Story of a Hedgehog Family* (London, 1972)

Reeve, Nigel, *Hedgehogs* (London, 1994)

Silver, Burton, *The Best of Bogor* (Wellington, 1994)

Standing Bear, Z. G., *The Gathering: Secretly Saving the World* (Bloomington, IN, 2007)

Wakeford, Tom, *Liaisons of Life: From Hornworts to Hippos, How the*

Unassuming Microbe Has Driven Evolution (Chichester, 2001)

Warwick, Hugh, *A Prickly Affair: The Charm of the Hedgehog* (London, 2008)

Wood, J. G., *Petland Revisited* (London, 1903)

Associations and Websites

CONSERVATION AND RESEARCH

BRITISH HEDGEHOG PRESERVATION SOCIETY (BHPS)
www.britishhedgehogs.org.uk

HEDGEHOG STREET
www.hedgehogstreet.org
Conservation project to create hedgehog habitat, run by the BHPS and
the People's Trust for Endangered Species

THE MAMMAL SOCIETY
www.mammal.org.uk
Study and conservation of mammals in the British Isles

PEOPLE'S TRUST FOR ENDANGERED SPECIES
www.ptes.org
British charity

PRO IGEL
www.pro-igel.de
Hedgehog conservation in Germany

WILDLIFE CONSERVATION RESEARCH UNIT
www.wildcru.org
Run by the Department of Zoology at the University of Oxford

DOMESTIC AND PET HEDGEHOGS

THE INTERNATIONAL HEDGEHOG ASSOCIATION
www.hedgehogclub.com

HEDGEHOG WELFARE SOCIETY
www.hedgehogwelfare.org
U.S. charity providing rescue services and care education

HEDGEHOG HOSPITALS IN THE UK

VALE WILDLIFE HOSPITAL AND REHABILITATION CENTRE
www.valewildlife.org.uk

TIGGYWINKLES
www.sttiggywinkles.org.uk

HESSILHEAD WILDLIFE RESCUE TRUST
www.hessilhead.org.uk

Acknowledgements

The pioneer of hedgehog research is Pat Morris and without his wisdom (and my occasional pilfering of it) this book would not have been possible. The staff at the British Hedgehog Preservation Society and the People's Trust for Endangered Species do so much to help this beleaguered icon. As do the hundreds of wildlife carers who sacrifice any hope of a social life as they nurse hedgehogs back to health. Ann Sylph at the wonderful library of the London Zoological Society helped enormously in tracking down images. And cartoonist Ed McLachlan was generous enough to redraw the image on page 192, as the original had been lost and was never scanned. Better still, he has given the new image to the BHPS. At Reaktion Books, Harry Gilonis was a great guide to the art of picture research and taught me never to unnecessarily CC an email, while Aimee Selby has shown me how a bit of elbow grease can make a lot of difference. My gorgeous family, Mati, Pip and Zoe, has supported me working on this project, managing to tolerate the influx of hedgehog artefacts flooding through the door. Final thanks, though, are due to *Erinaceus europaeus* – and in particular to a hedgehog called Nigel, who helped shift my perspective on the world.

Photo Acknowledgements

The author and publishers wish to express their thanks to the below sources of illustrative material and/or permission to reproduce it. Some locations are also given in the captions for the sake of brevity.

Aberdeen University Library: p. 50; photos courtesy the author: pp. 9, 10, 11, 12, 27, 41, 58, 134, 142, 144–5, 149, 151 (top), 153, 154, 159, 165, 170, 171, 172, 173, 174, 175, 179, 180, 181, 182, 191, 192; collection of the author: pp. 15 (foot), 16; photo Diane Balmer: p. 55; from Thomas Bell, *History of British Quadrupeds . . .* (London, 1837): p. 69; British Library, London: p. 59; photo British Library/Robana/Rex Features: p. 59; British Museum, London (photos © The Trustees of the British Museum): pp. 28, 32, 35 (foot), 36, 73, 78, 109, 128; from Lewis Carroll, *Alice's Adventures in Wonderland* (London, 1865): p. 84; reproduced courtesy of Celtic Marches Beverages Ltd: p. 79; by kind permission of Jim Collins and *Good to Great* (copyright © 2001): p. 104; by kind permission of Contintental Reifen Deutschland GmbH, Hanover: p. 135; photo Stormy Daniels: p. 114; from Ronald Dworkin, *Justice for Hedgehogs* (Cambridge, MA, 1977), reproduced by permission of Harvard University Press: p. 107; photo East News/Rex Features: p. 13; by kind permission of Alex Frecon: p. 119 (left); from *Die Gartenlaube* (Leipzig, 1878): p. 38; from Conrad Gesner, *Historia animalium libri I–IV . . . Lib. I: De quadrupedibus viviparis . . .* (Zürich, 1551): p. 68; photo Harke: p. 62; reproduced courtesy of *Hedgehog Review*: p. 103; by kind permission of Ken Howard: p. 122; photo Howey Hedgehog Rescue: p. 31; photo ImageBroker/Rex Features: p. 102; from Joannes Jonstonus, *Historiae*

Index

◆